GUIDE NIGHT SKIES
of Southern Africa

Peter Mack
Fellow of the Royal Astronomical Society

This book is dedicated to my wife, Josie

Published by Struik Nature
(an imprint of Random House Struik (Pty) Ltd)
Wembley Square, First Floor, Solan Road,
Cape Town, 8000
PO Box 1144, Cape Town, 8000 South Africa

Company Reg. No. 1966/003153/07

Visit us at **www.randomhousestruik.co.za**

First published in 1987 by Struik Publishers
Second edition (hardcover) 1989
Third edition 1995
Fourth edition 1996
This new edition 2012
10 9 8 7 6 5 4 3 2 1

Copyright © in text, 2012: Peter Mack
Copyright © in photographs, 2012: as indicated in captions to images
Copyright © in illustrations, 2012: Peter Mack
Star charts original source: TheSkyX © Software Bisque, Inc. All rights reserved.
Copyright © in published edition, 2012: Random House Struik (Pty) Ltd

Publisher: Pippa Parker
Managing editor: Helen de Villiers
Editors: Charles de Villiers, Emily Bowles
Designer: Janice Evans
Design assistant: Dominic Robson
Illustrator: James Berrangé
Proofreader: Tessa Kennedy
Indexer: Cora Ovens

Reproduction by Hirt & Carter Cape (Pty) Ltd
Printed and bound by Craft Print International Ltd, Singapore

All rights reserved. No part of this publication may be reproduced, stored in a retrieval system, or transmitted, in any form or by any means, electronic, mechanical, photocopying, recording or otherwise, without the prior written permission of the copyright owner(s).

978 177007 859 8 (Print ISBN)
978 143170 154 4 (ePub ISBN)
978 143170 155 1 (PDF ISBN)

Also available in Afrikaans as: *Gids tot die Naghemel van Suider-Afrika* (ISBN 978 1 77007 860 4)

Acknowledgements

I would like to thank the following people who provided materials and assistance: James McGaha, Bill Keel, Brian Murphy, Larry Cooper, Rene Burger, the staff at Cerro Tololo Inter-American Observatory, Chile, and the SARA Observatory.

Also the staff at Random House Struik, especially Emily Bowles, Janice Evans and Pippa Parker.

COVER: ***Composite photograph showing Comet Hale-Bopp – one of the brightest comets of the twentieth century.*** (The Biggerpicture/Photo Researchers)

PAGE 1: ***The Moon, Mercury and Venus seen over the dome of the South African Astronomical Observatory.*** (P. Mack)

PAGE 2: ***Just after Messenger's closest approach to Mercury, on 14 January 2008, the craft's narrow-angle camera obtained this image of the planet from a distance of 11 000 km. Craters as small as 1 km can be seen.*** (NASA/Johns Hopkins University Applied Physics Laboratory/Carnegie Institution of Washington)

CONTENTS

INTRODUCTION 4

BASIC ASTRONOMY 6
The constellations 6
The celestial sphere 7
Astronomical distances 10
How astronomers measure distance 11
How astronomers measure brightness 13
The electromagnetic spectrum 13
The astronomer's toolkit 14

THE SOLAR SYSTEM 18
The Sun 20
Planets 22
    Planetary positions 22
    Planetary motions 23
  Mercury 24
  Venus 26
  Earth 28
    The Moon 30
    Eclipses 32
  Mars 34
  Jupiter 36
  Saturn 40
  Uranus 42
  Neptune 43
Dwarf planets 46
  Pluto 47
  Eris 48
  Haumea 48
  Makemake 49
Ceres and the asteroid belt 50
Comets 51
Meteors 53
Other solar system phenomena 54
  Zodiacal light 54
  Aurorae 55

THE GALAXY 56
Stars 58
  Double stars 59
  Variable stars 60
Stellar evolution 62
Interstellar medium 64
  Nebulae 64
Star clusters 66

EXTRAGALACTIC ASTRONOMY 68
Galaxy classification 70
The expanding universe 72

STAR CHARTS 74
Selected interesting objects 92

APPENDIX 1: Mathematical expressions, constants and the Greek alphabet 98

APPENDIX 2: The constellations 99

APPENDIX 3: Data for the 30 brightest stars 100

APPENDIX 4: Planetary data 102

GLOSSARY 102

RESOURCES LIST 108

FURTHER READING 108

INDEX 109

INTRODUCTION

Astronomy is the oldest of all the sciences. It was more important in the life of man thousands of years ago than it is to the average person today. To ancient man, night-time was a frightening experience and he used to protect himself and allay his fears by staying close to an open fire. Imagine looking up at the starry skies thousands of years ago and trying to understand the universe. While the nature of the stars themselves was a mystery to those ancient observers, they realised that the rising of a particular group of stars, or constellation, heralded the onset of spring or winter, and bright stars were used for navigational purposes.

Most of the objects were known to be fixed stars, their relative positions remaining the same year after year. Observers from various civilisations arbitrarily split the stars into groups, or 'constellations'. Some, like the Ancient Greeks, thought they resembled mythological figures, animals or other creatures: Orion the hunter, and his dogs Canis Major and Canis Minor, the captured prey Lepus the hare, and so on. There were also a few wandering stars, which the Greeks called planets. These seemed to be confined to a path in the sky we call 'the ecliptic', and the early astronomers divided the stars along the path of the planets into the zodiacal constellations.

In time, astronomers learnt to predict the movement of these wandering stars. Together with the Sun and the Moon, they appeared to move around the Earth, which was considered to be at the centre of the universe. Occasionally, strange

A panorama of part of our galaxy, the Milky Way – a mystery to ancient observers. (John P. Gleason)

things would happen in the sky. A bright comet, which was generally believed to be a bad omen sent by an angry god, or a bright 'guest star' (supernova) might appear. When a partial solar eclipse occurred, the ancient Chinese believed that the Sun was being eaten by a dragon.

Modern astronomy is built upon thousands of years of knowledge, but the biggest advances have been made since the invention of the telescope in the first part of the seventeenth century, and above all in the last 60 years since the employment of computers and the advent of space exploration. One hundred years ago we were not sure what a galaxy was; 70 years ago radio astronomy was just being discovered; and just a few years ago we had only a sparse knowledge of the outer planets. This book will allow you to discover for yourself some of the many types of objects that make up the universe.

No previous knowledge of astronomy is required, but the reader will benefit from studying the book in some detail before going out to examine the sky. There is a small amount of mathematical notation such as powers of 10, and some astronomical abbreviations are used in the text, although these will be defined when they are first used. Should you encounter any unfamiliar terms, refer to the Glossary and Appendix 1 for explanations. Because of the rapid changes in technology, especially with digital cameras, today's advanced amateur astronomer can detect more objects than could the professional astronomer in the mid-twentieth century. Relatively low-cost computerised telescopes together with sophisticated software allow research to be conducted at a personal observatory. Astronomy is one of the few sciences where amateurs have made great contributions and will undoubtedly continue to do so in the future.

BASIC ASTRONOMY

THE CONSTELLATIONS

The modern constellation patterns have come to us largely from Ancient Greek astronomers. Additional constellations, mainly in the southern hemisphere, were added in the seventeenth century by Bayer, Hevelius and others, with some of the patterns named for modern instruments like the microscope and telescope. The rather faint and obscure constellation of Mensa is of local interest. It was originally named Mons Mensae ('Table Mountain') by La Caille, who formed the figure from the stars under the Large Magellanic Cloud (LMC), the name being suggested by Table Mountain in Cape Town, which was also frequently capped by cloud. It

Astronomers from different civilisations split stars into arbitrary constellations. (Crystalinks)

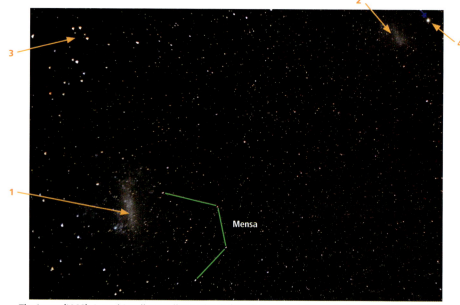

The Large (LMC), 1, and Small Magellanic Clouds (SMC), 2, are satellite galaxies to our own Milky Way. The four brightest stars in the constellation of Mensa are indicated. The bright group of stars to the upper left form the constellation of Reticulum, 3. The bright globular cluster NGC 104, better known as 47 Tucana, 4, and the Magellanic Clouds all reveal rich detail through binoculars. (P. Mack)

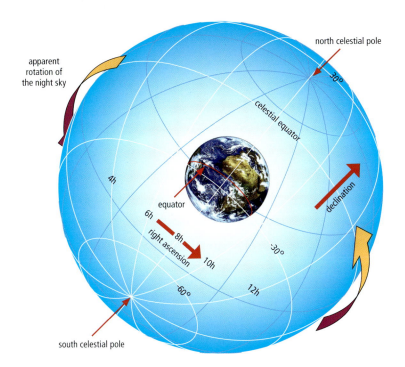

The lines of longitude and latitude on Earth have equivalent projections in the sky called lines of right ascension and declination. Just as one can find a place on Earth with co-ordinates, astronomers can use the equivalent lines to find objects in space, with the help of computerised telescopes.

is the only constellation named after a geographical feature on Earth.

There used to be a large number of constellations, but in 1922 the International Astronomical Union (IAU) pruned the list to make a total of 88. These are listed in Appendix 2. Only 30 or so of these constellations are easily recognisable – the majority are obscure and difficult to locate. Even most professional astronomers know only a handful of the constellations. Instead, they find objects by entering into a telescope's computer a set of co-ordinates similar to latitude and longitude on Earth. Most amateur astronomers, lacking such sophisticated equipment, find objects by matching the patterns in the sky to those represented in star charts, such as those given in this guide.

THE CELESTIAL SPHERE

Most people are familiar with the fundamental concepts of the poles and the lines of longitude and latitude on Earth. Astronomers have extended these ideas to facilitate 'navigation' of the night sky. Imagine that the Earth were placed at the centre of a huge hollow sphere that has the night sky painted on its inside surface. Suppose also that the Earth itself were a giant glass globe with lines of latitude and longitude marked on it, and a projection bulb placed at the centre. Then the shadows of those lines would be projected onto the inside of the enclosing sphere, which we term the 'celestial sphere'. This imaginary celestial sphere has poles aligned with the Earth's axis of rotation (and hence with the Earth's own poles), and an

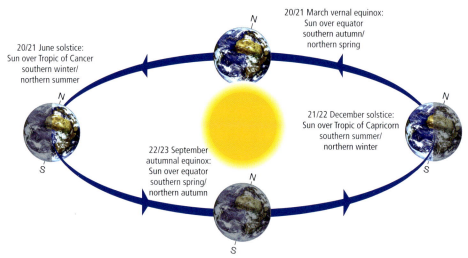

The seasons on Earth are not a result of the varying distance of the Earth from the Sun but rather the tilt of the Earth's rotational axis. Note that places on the equator receive an equal amount of daylight and darkness every day of the year.

equator in the same plane as the Earth's equator. The projections of the Earth's lines of longitude onto the celestial sphere are known as 'lines of right ascension' (RA), while the projections of the lines of latitude are called 'lines of declination'. Thus the celestial equator is at declination 0°, the north celestial pole is at declination +90° and the south celestial pole at -90°.

Lines of right ascension are measured in hours rather than degrees, where one hour corresponds to 15°, the angle through which the Earth rotates in 60 minutes. Zero hours RA is defined as the 'vernal equinox', the point where the Sun crosses the equator when 'moving' from south to north for the northern summer. Other points are measured eastwards of this. The vernal equinox used to be in the constellation of Aries, but it has since moved into the constellation of Pisces because of the 'precession' of the Earth's axis (see page 9).

All lines of RA are known as 'great circles'. By definition, a great circle divides the surface of a sphere into two equal halves (hemispheres). It is also the largest circle that fits on the sphere. The only line of declination that is a great circle is the equator, so-called because it splits the sphere into two equal halves. All other lines of declination are called 'small circles' and they become smaller towards the poles.

Because great circles divide the sphere into two equal halves, all great circles except the equator must intersect the equator at two points, opposite each other. A very important great circle is marked on almost all star charts, called 'the ecliptic'. It is tilted at an angle of about 23.5° to the equator and is the apparent path that the Sun traces out in the sky during the year as the Earth orbits the Sun. So by definition it is also the plane of the Earth's orbit. As mentioned, the point at which the Sun appears to cross the equator when moving from south to north is called the 'vernal equinox' and the opposite point is called the 'autumnal equinox'. The Sun reaches its northern limit in June and its southern limit in December. These declination limits were used by ancient astronomers to define the tropics of Capricorn and Cancer on Earth, so-called because the Sun reached its northern limit in the constellation of Cancer and its southern limit in Capricorn. Precession has since caused these northern and southern limits to move into the constellations of Gemini and Sagittarius respectively.

All of the planets' orbits around the Sun are closely confined to a single disc or plane. So, as seen from Earth, all of the planets appear to follow the path of the ecliptic, never deviating by more than 9° on either side. The inclination of the Moon's orbit to the ecliptic is just over 5°, so it too is always close to this path.

The location of a city on Earth can be given as a pair of co-ordinates (latitude and longitude). By definition the zero longitude runs through the Greenwich Observatory east of London. For Cape Town the co-ordinates are (33°58' S, 18°36' E). A similar scheme is used to catalogue the positions of stars and other celestial objects; but these are always given in the form (right ascension, declination). For instance, the brightest star in the sky, Sirius, has co-ordinates (RA = 6 hours, 45 minutes, dec. = -16°43'). Recall that there are 24 hours in a day and 360° in a circle. So one hour of time is the equivalent of 15°, and one minute of time is the equivalent of a quarter of a degree. The declination of Sirius is read as 'minus 16 degrees 43 minutes'. Here a degree is split into 60 equal parts called 'minutes of arc', which are not related to minutes of time. Advanced amateur telescopes are now equipped with computers and motors allowing them to be automatically pointed at stars using this co-ordinate system.

The gravitational attraction of the Sun and the Moon on the Earth's equatorial bulge results in a slow movement of the Earth's axis of rotation about a central line, like a spinning top that is just about to topple. The celestial pole traces out a circle on the celestial sphere 47° in diameter, taking 25 800 years to return to the same point. Thus the pole stars of today are quite different from those seen in antiquity. This 'precession of the equinoxes' causes an apparent westward migration of all the lines on the celestial sphere, so that the equinoxes move west by about 50 arc seconds per annum.

The ecliptic or path of the Sun is marked on most star charts and in the course of the year, because of the Earth's tilted axis, the Sun moves between 23.5° north and 23.5° south of the equator.

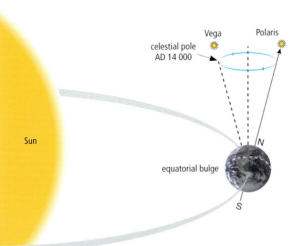

Precession of the equinoxes: the gravitational pull of the Sun and the Moon causes the Earth's rotational axis to wobble over a period of 25 800 years. This changes the alignment of the stars so that Vega, not Polaris, will be close to the north celestial pole 14 000 years from now.

ASTRONOMICAL DISTANCES

Astronomical distances are so enormous as to be beyond the grasp of most people. The distance from Earth to the Sun is 149 597 870 km, and astronomers call this one 'astronomical unit' (AU).

The distance to Neptune, the outermost planet of our solar system, is approximately 30 AU, and the nearest star is over 271 000 AU distant. Let us now construct a scale model of the local astronomical environment, out to the distance of the nearest star. Suppose we were to shrink the Earth down until it is precisely 3 mm in diameter. At this scale the Sun would be about the size of a beach ball, 327 mm in diameter. The first planet out from the Sun, Mercury, would be positioned 13.6 m away, a ball just over 1 mm in diameter. Venus would be almost the same size as the Earth, 25 m out, and the Earth would be positioned 35 m from the Sun. The Moon, now shrunk down to a mere 0.8 mm, would orbit the Earth at a distance of 90 mm. The red planet, Mars, approximately twice the size of the Moon, would be located 54 m from the Sun.

Next come the giants of the solar system. Jupiter and Saturn would each be about the size of a Ping-Pong ball, 183 m and 336 m away respectively. Uranus would be 675 m away and Neptune just over 1 km away. The distance to the dwarf planet Pluto varies considerably, but let us place it 1.4 km away from the Sun on our scale model. One noticeable feature of the solar system is that the distance between the planets is enormous compared to their diameters: most of the space is empty. Comets can move much further out, to over 2 000 km on our model, and the distance to the nearest star would be over 9 500 km – remember that the diameter of the Earth was shrunk to just 3 mm.

The dimensions of a galaxy are so large that, even using this scale model, we would end up talking in hundreds of millions of kilometres, which is again an incomprehensible distance.

Light travels very quickly, at a speed equivalent to going seven times around the Earth in one second. Yet the Sun's light takes approximately 8 minutes to reach us, and the light from Proxima Centauri, the nearest star besides the Sun, takes over 4 years to make the journey. Proxima Centauri is therefore said to be over four 'light years' away. The diameter of our own Galaxy is 100 000 light years: that is, light from a star on one side of the Galaxy will take 100 000 years to reach a star on the opposite side. These distances may seem

Astronomical distances	
Destination	**Estimated time of arrival**
Earth's Moon	9.6 seconds
Planet Mars	1.59 hours
Planet Saturn	9.98 hours
Dwarf planet Pluto	1.71 days
Closest star to the Sun (Proxima Centauri)	31.5 years
Centre of the Milky Way Galaxy	22 000 years
Closest large spiral galaxy (Andromeda)	1.9 million years
Coma cluster of galaxies	2.5 billion years
Edge of the observable universe	50 billion years

This table indicates how long it would take you to reach various objects in the solar system and beyond, if you were travelling at 40 000 km·s^{-1} – the speed required to travel around the Earth in one second.

beyond comprehension, yet as we shall soon discover, they are nevertheless tiny in the scale of the universe.

Modern astronomers do not use light years as a unit of distance measurement. Instead they use parsecs (abbreviation: pc), where one parsec is 3.26 light years. What is the source of this strange number? It is the distance from the Sun at which the radius of the Earth's orbit would subtend an angle of one arc second.

HOW ASTRONOMERS MEASURE DISTANCE

Astronomers measure distance in various ways. The first technique used was that of parallax, which is the same method used by surveyors on Earth. It is easy to demonstrate the principle. Hold up a finger at arm's length, close one eye, and note the position against the distant background. Now view with the other eye. As you blink each eye in turn, the finger appears to move against the more distant background objects. The stars are very far away, so the distance between the two viewing points needs to be as large as possible. So measurements are made approximately 6 months apart, on opposite sides of the Earth's orbit, to provide the longest possible baseline.

The first parallax measurements were made in the early nineteenth century. Using this method, astronomers could measure the distance only to relatively nearby stars, because for distant stars the change in angle would be too small to measure. They had already noted that some stars appeared to be moving relative to all the other stars that were 'fixed' (astronomers call this 'proper motion'), so these apparently moving stars were likely to be closer. Also the brightest stars were likely to be closest. Thomas

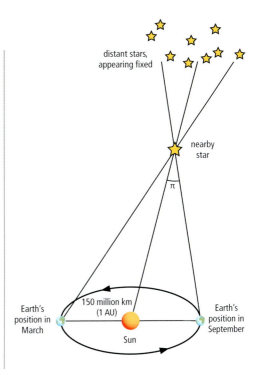

The apparent position of a nearby star against very distant stars changes as the Earth orbits the Sun. By viewing a nearby star from opposite sides of the Earth's orbit the very small angle (π) can be measured and hence the distance determined by trigonometry.

Henderson, working from South Africa, made measurements of Alpha Centauri (one of the brightest stars). He finished in 1833 and went back to England with his data. He had only 19 measurements, and his instrument had been damaged in shipping. He applied corrections to accommodate for the damage but realised that others would cast doubt on his work, so he decided to wait for a better instrument, and made another trip back. As we now know, Alpha Centauri is indeed one of the closest stars (it's actually part of a triple star system of which Proxima Centauri is the closest). Moreover, Henderson's calculations turned out to be largely correct. In the

The Hipparcos satellite made parallax observations until 1993, accurately charting 118 218 stars. (European Space Agency (ESA))

Moon against the stars, Hipparchus was able to determine the Moon's parallax and thus its distance from the Earth. He also made the first accurate star map, which led to the discovery of the precession of the equinoxes (see page 9).

Different methods are used for measuring stars at different distances. For relatively nearby stars, say up to 10 pc away, trigonometrical parallax can be used. This is the same technique land surveyors use on Earth, but the 'baseline' is the diameter of the Earth's orbit. Nowadays orbiting satellites are used to measure distances of a few hundred parsecs.

For distances within our own Galaxy, variable stars (those whose brightness varies with time) are often used. For Cepheid and Mira variables (hot super-giant and very cool red giant stars) there is a relationship that connects the time interval between successive maxima in the light curve, and the inherent luminosity of the star. Thus, by measuring the period of variability, the true luminosity can be found, and knowing this together with the apparent luminosity as seen from Earth, the distance can be deduced.

Measurements to the more distant galaxies are usually made by observing the redshift of the object. When an object moves away from us, features in its spectrum are displaced towards longer (redder) wavelengths. The more distant the galaxy, the greater the redshift, and the faster away it is moving, an effect known as 'Hubble's law'.

meantime the German astronomer Friedrich Wilhelm Bessel had obtained a far superior instrument and in 1838 observed the star 61 Cygni, known to have a rapid motion against the background stars. He measured its distance as 3.18 pc, rather close to the modern value of 3.49 pc. In recognition of his work, 61 Cygni is also known as 'Bessel's Star'.

Parallax measurements are no longer made from ground-based observatories. In 1989 the European Space Agency launched the Hipparcos satellite, which made parallax observations until 1993. Measurements made with the main instrument charted 118 218 stars with ultra-high precision. A second instrument made measurements of lesser but still unprecedented accuracy, bringing the total to 2 539 913 stars. 'Hipparcos' is an acronym for HIgh Precision PARallax COllecting Satellite. Appropriately the pronunciation is also very close to that of Hipparchus, the name of a Greek astronomer who lived from 190 to 120 BC. By measuring the position of the

HOW ASTRONOMERS MEASURE BRIGHTNESS

Even the most casual glance at the night sky will reveal that stars and planets are of different brightness. This can occur for two reasons: the objects are at different distances and/or they really are of different absolute brightness. A system for measuring the brightness of stars was first introduced by the ancient Greek astronomer Hipparchus, and later refined by the English astronomer Pogson after the invention of logarithms, and the basic unit was called 'a magnitude' (abbreviated to mag). The brightest stars in the sky were assigned mag 0 and the faintest ones seen by the unaided eye, mag 6. A difference of five magnitudes corresponds to a difference in brightness of 100. The system has been refined marginally since then so that now the brightest stars are approximately mag -1 and Venus is mag -4. The two brightest objects in the sky are the Sun at mag -26 and the Full Moon at mag -12. The largest telescopes in the world can detect objects approaching mag 30, which is 1 000 million times fainter than the eye can see.

In order to get a fair comparison of one object with another, astronomers also calculate the magnitude the objects would have if they were placed at the same fixed distance away from us. This standard distance is 10 pc or 32.6 light years, and the figures are then referred to as absolute magnitudes.

THE ELECTROMAGNETIC SPECTRUM

The human eye can only detect visible light, which is a tiny portion of the electromagnetic spectrum. If we observe an object in visible light alone, we do not necessarily get a representative picture.

'Modern' astronomy started when astronomers began to explore wavelengths outside the visible spectrum, starting with the radio spectrum, just after World War II. Great advances have been made in infrared, microwave, ultraviolet, X-ray and gamma-ray astronomy, with observations made from rockets and artificial satellites high above Earth's atmosphere.

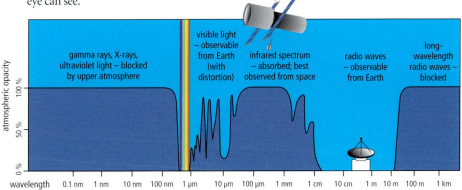

The electromagnetic spectrum covers the entire range of detectable wavelengths. Think of a wavelength as the distance between the two crests of a swell in the ocean. The horizontal axis in this diagram represents wavelengths varying from the size of an atomic nucleus to many kilometres. The visible wavelengths are only a tiny fraction of the whole spectrum. For astronomers to understand the astrophysics of objects they need to look at the full spectrum, which requires space-based observatories.

THE ASTRONOMER'S TOOLKIT

This book is designed for the newcomer to astronomy, and so most of the objects we discuss are visible to the naked eye or with a pair of binoculars. However, most amateur astronomers yearn to own a telescope and other sophisticated equipment, so let's take a look at an astronomer's tools.

Although the professional astronomer uses highly sophisticated electronic devices to detect objects, the casual amateur astronomer relies on the human eye as the primary detector. The eye partly adapts itself to very low light levels by increasing the size of the pupil. You can easily demonstrate this by standing in front of a mirror and closing your eyes for about 30 seconds. While your eyes are closed your pupils open to let more light in. Now open your eyes and watch the pupils rapidly close to limit the amount of light getting in. The retina also has chemical activity to help it cope with brighter conditions, and this takes some time to dissipate.

It is important to acquire dark adaptation before serious observing by remaining in a dark environment for about 10 minutes. During this time the pupils will open to about 6 or 7 mm in diameter. If the eye is subjected to a bright light then the dark adaptation will be ruined and a further 10 minutes must elapse before serious observing can begin. Complete dark adaptation of the eye (starting from daylight) may take up to 40 minutes.

Red light is the least damaging to dark adaptation, so if you need a torch make sure that it has a red filter. However, within a few minutes of being outside with no artificial lights, you will notice a substantial improvement in your vision.

Binoculars are perhaps the most underrated piece of equipment in an astronomer's toolkit, being, in effect, a

Magnification is the least important parameter in a telescope: the magnification used on the world's largest telescopes is approximately the same as that used in modest amateur telescopes. (P. Mack)

portable pair of telescopes. Two basic designs of binoculars are available, 'Galilean' or opera glasses and the more modern 'prismatic' binoculars, which are far better suited to astronomy. They are available in different sizes and are normally designated by two numbers, such as 7×30 or 10×50. The first number refers to the magnification and the second to the aperture size or diameter of the front lens in millimetres. Dividing the second number by the first gives the diameter of the exit pupil, so for both 7×35 and 10×50 binoculars, the exit pupil diameter is 5 mm. The maximum diameter that the eye can accept is approximately 6 mm when fully dark-adapted. The bigger the aperture the more light will be collected and the brighter the image will appear. Increasing the magnification will make the image appear dimmer for a given aperture size and will limit the field of view. Besides this, if the binoculars are hand-held the objects dance around because of vibrations in the hand. The latter problem can be overcome by using a sturdy tripod with braced legs.

A number of camera stores stock larger aperture binoculars such as 10×80, 15×80 and 20×80, all of which are very heavy. Only the 15×80 binoculars would be of use in astronomy because the 10× magnification results in an exit pupil size of 8 mm, which is larger than the eye can accept, while the 20× model gives a very limited view of the sky, making objects difficult to find. Certain manufacturers also make 'zoom binoculars' where the magnification can be changed with a rotating lever. These are totally unsuitable for astronomy. The optimum combination is probably 10×50 binoculars mounted on a tripod. This will outperform many of the cheaper telescopes of flimsy construction.

There are three main types of telescope on two basic types of mounting. The 'refractor' uses a lens to bend (refract) the light to a focus, a 'Newtonian reflector' uses a concave parabolic mirror, and a 'catadioptric reflector' uses a combination of both lenses and mirrors. Magnification is the least important parameter in a telescope: the magnification used on the world's largest telescopes is approximately the same as that used in modest amateur

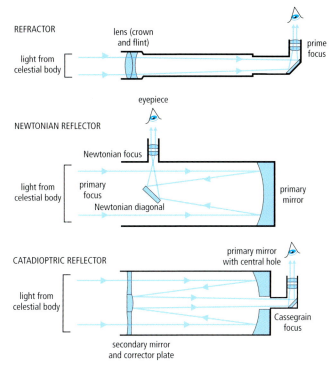

Three common types of telescope used by amateur astronomers.

BASIC ASTRONOMY 15

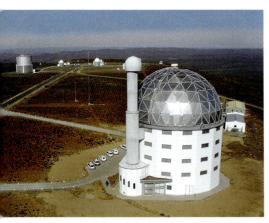

An aerial view of the Southern African Large Telescope (SALT), which uses a 10 m reflector. This is one of the largest optical telescopes in the southern hemisphere. (Jeremy Duffy/Helicam)

telescopes. Light-gathering power and resolution are the critical factors in telescope performance and these improve if one uses a bigger lens or mirror, which is why professional astronomers use such large telescopes.

Let's now consider the two basic mounting configurations for telescopes. The first is an 'equatorial' design where one of the axes is aligned parallel to the Earth's axis of rotation. By fully turning the telescope on this axis once every 24 hours the effect of the Earth's rotation can be cancelled. This type of mounting is very popular on sophisticated amateur equipment and most small professional telescopes, up to a few metres in diameter. The other type of mounting is the 'Alt-Az', short for 'altitude and azimuth', the two directions in which the axes move. The telescope must be moved in a stepped pattern to follow the rising and setting arcs of a celestial body. With the advent of computer technology this mounting is regaining popularity, because it has considerable advantages from a structural engineering viewpoint. The largest optical telescope in the world uses this type of mounting, as do most radio telescopes. Surprisingly, many cheap unstable telescopes are also of this design, which should be avoided at all costs for manual use. An exception is the Dobsonian design, which can easily be made at home with simple hand tools.

Modern advanced amateur telescopes are available in both styles of mount. They are equipped with a GPS system to allow portable devices to determine the observing site accurately. With minimal effort these telescopes can be used to find thousands of objects (including the Moon and planets) from catalogues stored in the onboard computer.

This is the second largest telescope in southern Africa: its mirror is 1.9 m in diameter. It was built between 1938 and 1948 for the Radcliffe Observatory, Pretoria, and is now at Sutherland. (South African Astronomical Observatory (SAAO))

If you intend purchasing or making a telescope (a task that is not as difficult as it may sound), then it would be wise to contact your local astronomical society first. You can look through their telescopes and decide on your own personal requirements – besides which, astronomy is much more fun if you can discuss your findings with other people.

Astronomical photography is one of the best ways to present your observations, and many years later an accurate and unbiased account will still be available. Some of the photographs presented in this publication were taken by the author using a very simple set-up comprising a digital camera and a tripod. The type of camera required is a 'DSLR' or digital single-lens reflex camera. The lenses are interchangeable and the shutter settings, sensitivity (the equivalent of film speed) and other parameters can be set manually. Using a tripod, the maximum exposure time is less than one minute, as otherwise the stars 'trail'. Simple tracking mechanisms are also available. These modern cameras can take images in colour or black and white. Astronomers often take three 'black and white' images through red, green and blue filters to create a colour image. However, several of the images presented in this book were simple 'point and shoot' exposures made with a Canon camera.

Digital cameras use a charge-coupled device (CCD) detector, which is similar to the device used at large professional observatories. The size of the detector varies between models, as a larger detector costs more. However, two different camera models from the same manufacturer will use the same lens. If one detector is twice the size of another, then for a given lens it will see twice as much.

Lenses are specified by two parameters, the focal length and the focal ratio or f/ratio. The shorter the focal length, the wider the field of view. The smaller (faster) the f/ratio for a given focal length, the more light is let in. So a fast f/ratio is ideal for astronomy. Fast optics are harder to manufacture and tend to be more expensive. The f/ratio of the lens can be changed. Unfortunately, low-quality lenses show all their defects when set to the smallest f/ratio and can render very poor pictures: a lens that gives perfectly adequate portrait and landscape pictures may turn out to be unsatisfactory for astronomical work. The problem can be overcome by closing down the aperture stop, but this lets in less light, and so longer exposures are required.

Very pleasing images can be obtained by using wide-angle lenses (15 mm focal length). Generally, fixed lenses rather than zoom lenses give the best quality images. A 30-second exposure with a professional Canon camera, for example, will show fine detail in the Milky Way. Of course, it is necessary to travel away from the bright city lights to obtain these images.

Let us now take stock and summarise an astronomer's toolkit. If you have a limited budget then a telescope is almost certainly out of the question for the moment. The first outlay should be for a good pair of binoculars. If possible go to a reputable shop that specialises in astronomy. The second purchase should be a very sturdy braced tripod. A good tripod will repay its cost time and time again, both in binocular and photographic observations. A digital camera should probably be the next purchase. Finally, consider a telescope, but only after consulting your local astronomical society.

THE SOLAR SYSTEM

The solar system is defined as that volume of space that contains objects that are captured by the Sun's gravitational field. It extends out approximately half of the way to the nearest stars and contains the planets and their numerous satellites, as well as dwarf planets, comets, asteroids and interplanetary material such as meteors and dust. The Sun accounts for nearly all of the mass in the solar system, and almost all of the remainder is contained in the planets, whose orbits are almost circular and lie within a flat disc that is coincident with the Sun's equator. The planets were formed out of material that was contained in this disc some 4.6 billion years ago.

The advent of unmanned interplanetary travel has completely revolutionised our knowledge of the planets. Probes have landed on the surfaces of Venus, Mars, Titan (a moon of Saturn) and the asteroid Eros, and have taken close-up pictures of all the planets and their moons.

We now know that our solar system is not unique: astronomers have discovered hundreds of extra-solar planets orbiting nearby stars. They have also recently

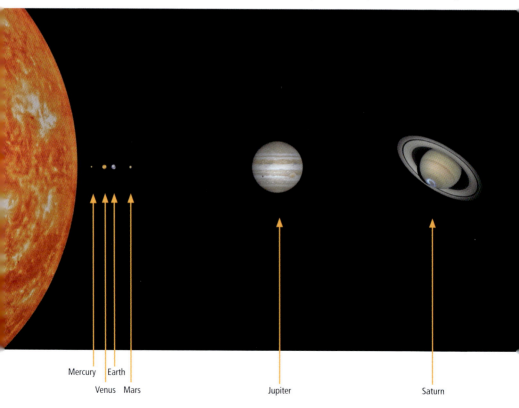

redefined objects in our solar system (see page 46), and now recognise only eight planets, which are, in distance order from the Sun: Mercury, Venus, Earth, Mars, Jupiter, Saturn, Uranus and Neptune. Pluto is now defined as a dwarf planet.

There are five known dwarf planets: Ceres (which lies in the asteroid belt between Mars and Jupiter), Pluto, Eris, Haumea and Makemake. These last four objects all lie beyond Neptune and are also called 'plutoids', a plutoid being a type of trans-Neptunian object (TNO). Planets have orbital planes close to the plane of the Sun's equator, but dwarf planets can have highly inclined orbits. Six of the planets and three dwarf planets are orbited by natural satellites, usually called 'moons'. These systems can be complex. The very edge of the solar system is thought to contain a vast reservoir of long-period comets.

Solar system astronomy is a specialised subject. Historically, astronomers studying the solar system have had only a minor interest in objects further afield, but this is changing as more extra-solar planets are discovered.

The inner four planets are called 'terrestrial planets' because they have a similar composition to that of Earth. The outer four, called the 'gas giants', are massive and comprise mainly frozen gases. This montage shows the relative diameters of the planets to scale, but greatly compresses the distances between them.

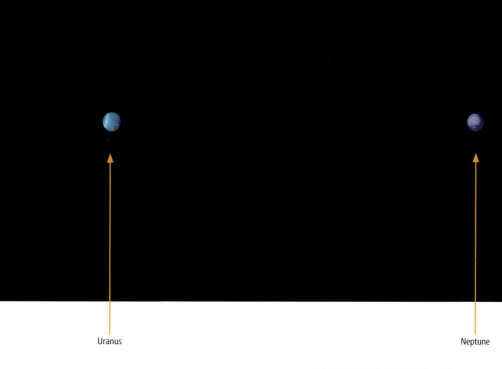

Uranus

Neptune

THE SOLAR SYSTEM 19

THE SUN

The Sun is our very own star, sustaining life on Earth through the light and heat that it constantly emits. It is vital to our existence, but apart from its proximity to Earth there is nothing special about this star. Indeed, the Sun is a typical middle-aged star. It has a mass of 2×10^{30} kg, some 333 000 times that of the Earth and about 99.86% of the total mass of the solar system. Astronomers use the mass and luminosity of the Sun as a standard against which to measure other objects outside the solar system. The Sun is entirely gaseous, an enormous ball comprised chiefly of incandescent hydrogen. This nuclear furnace converts about 5×10^9 kg of hydrogen fuel into helium every second, and thus generates in a second more than the total amount of energy that humans have ever used. Even using up fuel at this enormous rate, the change in the mass of the Sun while it is 'burning' hydrogen will be less than 0.1%. The nuclear reactions take place deep in its interior, in a region known as the 'core', where the temperature is around 1.57×10^6 °C. The core extends out to a quarter of the radius, which is only 1.5% of the volume of the Sun, but it contains half of the mass. When the Sun formed out of interstellar gas about 5×10^9 years ago, the core consisted of about 75% hydrogen, almost 25% helium and about 1% of the heavier elements. The outer part of the Sun still has this composition, but the core has changed due to the nuclear reactions going on there. The core has been burning nuclear fuel for over 4.5×10^9 years and the hydrogen abundance has fallen to 35% as much of it has been converted into helium, which now accounts for around 65% of the core mass.

There are no permanent features on the Sun because of its gaseous nature, but it does have sunspots: relatively cool, dark areas on its surface that can grow to be many times larger than the area of the Earth. They were known to ancient Chinese astronomers who observed them with the naked eye when the Sun was partly obscured by cloud. Sunspots are associated with magnetic fields and flares. They vary in number from almost none at minimum, when they occur towards the solar poles, to several dozen or more at maximum, when they appear nearer the

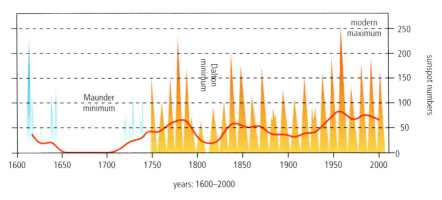

The number of sunspots visible on the solar disc varies over an 11-year period. The actual number of spots at maximum varies. In the 1600s the Sun was in a very quiescent stage, and recent data suggests that we may be entering another minimum.

equator, the cycle repeating every 11 years. The 2011/12 maximum was very weak and the Sun may be entering a quiescent phase. Reliable sunspot counts have been obtained since around 1750. Data available before then suggests a minimum lasting half a century when almost no spots were visible. This 'Maunder minimum' correlates with the mini ice age of the Middle Ages. The modern maximum may be contributing to the global warming effect, although most of the current warming is due to greenhouse gas emissions.

The Sun spins on its own axis with a mean period of 25.38 days and some of the larger sunspots can persist for more than one rotation. To examine sunspots, focus your binoculars on a distant terrestrial object (church spire, etc.), then remove them from your eyes and point the large lenses towards the Sun, holding a piece of white card a few centimetres from the eyepiece. When the binoculars cast the smallest shadow on the card, they are pointing in the right direction. The light then emerging from the eyepiece will project an image of the Sun, and any sunspots and flares, inside the shadow on the card. You can also use the type of set-up illustrated to the right.

The Sun is important to astronomers as it is the only star we can study in detail. Not even the world's largest telescope will show another star as a disc. About 20% of the world's astronomers study the Sun full-time and a large number of amateurs make it their speciality.

Sunspots and faculae can be safely observed by projecting an image of the Sun using a pair of binoculars and a shade box. A piece of paper with a hole cut in it fits over one of the binocular lenses (top arrow), creating a shadow to block stray light. A hole 3 to 4 cm in diameter is cut in the shade box (lower arrow) and a viewing aperture cut in one side. Using higher magnification binoculars or a longer projection distance will result in a larger image. (P. Mack)

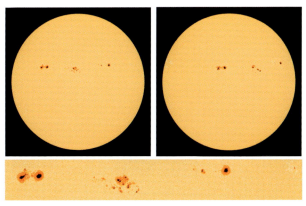

Images taken two days apart showing the rotation of the solar disc from left to right. The bottom strip shows details of the sunspots, which change on a scale of just hours. (NASA/Solar Dynamics Observatory (SDO))

PLANETS

All of the planets orbit the Sun in the same direction, counter-clockwise as viewed from above the Sun's north pole. They are also confined to a narrow plane centred on the Sun's equator. Their apparent path through the sky is a result of their own orbital motion and that of the observer on Earth. Apart from the two 'inferior' (inner) planets, Mercury and Venus, they normally appear to move slowly from west to east against the stars. However, the relatively rapid motion of the Earth along its orbital path gives the appearance that they first rise in the east and slowly migrate westwards over the seasons.

The path of Mars across the sky is most informative, because it exhibits the largest retrograde (backward) motion with respect to the Earth. This feature, combined with the large variation in the distance of Mars from the Earth, allowed Kepler to solve the problem of planetary motions.

The inferior planets appear to rise from the direction of the rising or setting Sun and then fall back again after about 20 days in the case of Mercury and 105 days in the case of Venus. Most noticeable is the easterly movement of the Moon – approximately 12° per day, resulting in the Moon rising approximately 45 minutes later each day.

PLANETARY POSITIONS

The angle between the Sun and a planet as viewed from Earth is called its 'elongation'. A superior planet is in conjunction when its elongation is 0° and it is positioned on the opposite side of the Sun to the Earth (and is hence not visible). When they are again in a straight line, but with the Earth between the Sun and the planet, the elongation is 180° and opposition occurs. This is the best time to view the planet as it is much closer and it transits at midnight. There are two positions in the orbit of a superior planet called 'quadrature', when the elongation is exactly 90°.

For an inferior planet the position on the far side of the Sun, when all three bodies are in a straight line, is called 'superior conjunction', while the case when the planet lies between the Earth and the Sun is called 'inferior conjunction'. The point at which the Sun-Earth-Planet angle reaches a maximum is called the 'greatest elongation', and this is one of the best times for observation. The Moon is said to be 'in syzygy' when in conjunction (New) or opposition (Full).

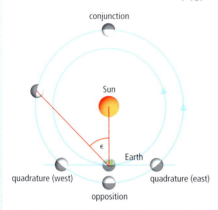

Orbit of a superior planet – at 90° elongation the planet is at quadrature; at 180° elongation it is opposite the Sun, highest in the sky at midnight, and best placed for observation.

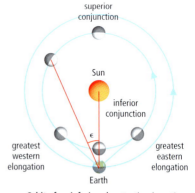

Orbit of an inferior planet – the elongation (Sun-Earth-Planet angle ϵ) can never exceed 47°. At greatest eastern elongation the planet is visible in the morning sky.

PLANETARY MOTIONS

Early astronomers observed but did not understand the motions of the planets against the stars (planet is Greek for 'wanderer'). Ptolemy believed that Earth was the centre of the universe and that other objects revolved around it in circular orbits, and so a complex model was needed to explain why the motions of planets varied in speed and direction. In 1543 Copernicus risked his life by publishing his revolutionary and heretical ideas, which demoted the Earth from the centre of the universe, proposing instead that the planets revolved around the Sun, although he retained the system of epicycles, which held that the planets moved in independent circles.

Danish nobleman Tycho Brache accurately observed the planets' positions, particularly Mars. After his death in 1601 his assistant Johannes Kepler noted that these observations of Mars didn't fit a circular orbit whether it was placed around the Earth or the Sun. He concluded that the planets move in ellipses around the Sun. (Note that a circle is a special case of an ellipse with eccentricity of zero.) Kepler formulated three laws of planetary motion that in fact apply to most objects orbiting the Sun.

Kepler's laws

1. The planets move in elliptical orbits, with the Sun at one focus while the other focus is empty.
2. The line joining the planet to the Sun sweeps out equal areas in equal times.
3. The square of the period of revolution of a planet around the Sun is proportional to the cube of the ellipse's semi-major axis (half of the distance A-B). This final law was announced in 1619.

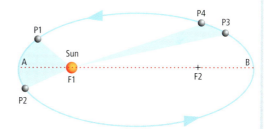

The area P1-P2-F1 is equal to the area P3-P4-F1 and the planet or other solar system body takes the same time to travel between P1 and P2 as it does going from P3 to P4.

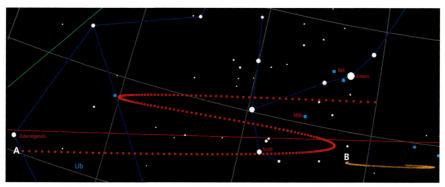

The paths that Mars and Saturn will appear to take during the 2016 opposition: Mars moves clockwise from left to right starting at point A; Saturn moves counter-clockwise starting at point B. (The solid red line shows the path of the ecliptic.)

☿ Mercury

Mercury, the smallest planet in the solar system, is only 0.055 times the mass of the Earth. Being closest to the Sun it also has the shortest orbital period – 88 days – and the shortest synodic period (interval between closest approaches to Earth) – 116 days. So it alternates between the morning and evening sky seven times a year. Seen from the Earth, its angular distance from the Sun, or elongation, never exceeds 28°, so it rises or sets within 2 hours of the Sun. Thus it can only be seen in the bright twilight sky in the west just after sunset or in the east just before sunrise. Of the five planets known to the ancients Mercury is the most difficult to find, because of its proximity to the Sun.

The best viewing conditions occur when the ecliptic is at a steep angle to the horizon, which, from the southern hemisphere, is during March and April (morning appearance) and September and October (evening appearance). In unfavourable years the spring and autumn elongations can be very small, around 18°. Mercury has the most eccentric orbit of all the planets: its eccentricity is 0.21 with its distance from the Sun ranging from 46 to 70 million km.

A remarkable feature of Mercury is its rapid movement against the background stars. It is mostly too close to the Sun to be observed, but can normally be seen for a few weeks at a time in the morning sky and a few weeks in the evening sky. It is brightest at the start of the observation window when in the evening sky, and brightest at the end of the observation window when in the morning sky. Binoculars will help you find the planet, although a disc will not be visible. It looks like a brilliant orange to yellowish star, the brightness reaching mag -2.3. A small telescope will show the tiny disc, which varies in size between 2 and 12 arc seconds and exhibits a phase between almost full and a thick crescent.

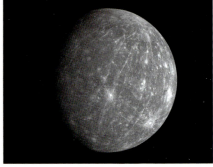

Mercury as imaged by Messenger. (NASA/Johns Hopkins University Applied Physics Laboratory/Carnegie Institution of Washington)

This view of the impact crater Degas was obtained by the Messenger spacecraft orbiting Mercury. The crater (52 km in diameter) cooled just after it formed and the floor cracked. The insert shows the same crater as imaged during the Mariner 10 flyby. (NASA/Johns Hopkins University Applied Physics Laboratory/Carnegie Institution of Washington)

The orbit of Mercury is inclined at 7° to the ecliptic so normally it passes north or south of the Sun. However, Mercury can transit the solar disc when all three bodies (the Sun, Mercury and Earth) come into the same plane. This is only possible when Mercury cuts through the plane of the ecliptic, within a few days of 7 May or 9 November. May transits occur at intervals of 13 and 46 years while November transits occur more often, at intervals of 7, 13 and 46 years. The transit lasts for about 5 or 6 hours and is visible if the Sun is above the horizon. The next two transits, in 2016 and 2019, will both be visible from Africa. Use

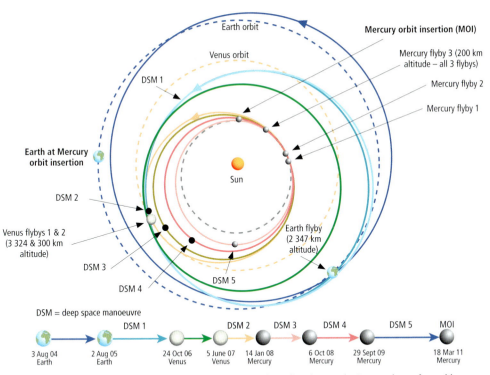

Messenger entered Mercury's orbit in March 2011. The planet lies close to the Sun, so the craft would have accelerated too quickly during its approach for a successful orbit insertion; the planet also has no atmosphere to reduce velocity. Since deceleration would have required too much fuel, a series of flybys was instead used to slow the craft. Messenger has been measuring the solar wind on its journey.

EARLY TWENTY-FIRST CENTURY TRANSITS	
2003: 7 May	2006: 8 Nov
2016: 9 May	2019: 11 Nov
	2039: 7 Nov
2049: 7 May	2052: 9 Nov

the same technique to see the transit as for observing sunspots (page 21).

There is no atmosphere on Mercury and the temperature conditions are extreme: 350 °C during the day and -170 °C at night. For almost a century, astronomers thought that Mercury always presented the same face to the Sun, just as the Moon does to the Earth. Radar observations made in 1965 showed that this is not so: a day on Mercury lasts 58.65 Earth days and the sidereal period (the time taken to orbit the Sun) is 88 days. Thus Mercury is in a 3:2 spin-orbit resonance. This means that a day on Mercury lasts for two-thirds of an orbital period, and after two orbital periods the same face is again presented to the Sun.

Despite its small size (diameter 4 880 km) and slow rotation period, Mercury has a strong magnetic field, about 1.1 times that of Earth, implying that it has a large, rich iron core. Its density of 5.43 g·cm³ is the second highest in the solar system, after Earth (5.52 g·cm³). Its surface, heavily cratered by meteoric bombardment in the early life of the solar system, looks rather like that of the Moon but lacks the large 'seas' of basalt lava flows. Mercury has been geologically dormant for at least 4 000 million years or about 90% of its life.

♀ Venus

Venus is the closest planet to the Earth. This factor, together with its proximity to the Sun, makes Venus the most conspicuous of all the planets and the brightest object in the sky after the Sun and the Moon. It is often referred to as the 'evening star' when in the west or as the 'morning star' when in the east, and it is so bright that it can actually cast a shadow when the Moon and artificial light sources are absent.

Venus is approximately twice as far from the Sun as Mercury, so it can be seen for much longer intervals, typically seven months at each elongation. The maximum angular distance, or greatest elongation, from the Sun is 47°. Thus Venus rises or sets no more than 3 hours, 13 minutes before sunrise or after sunset respectively, implying that it can only be seen for a maximum of 2 hours in a dark sky.

A radar map of Venus from the orbiting Magellan probe reveals a variety of surface features such as mountains, canyons, valleys and level ground. Smooth plains comprise about 60% of the ground, from which rise numerous volcanoes, ranging from 0.5 to 1 500 km in diameter.
(NASA/Magellan Project/Jet Propulsion Laboratory (JPL))

The phases of Venus are more pronounced than those of Mercury and can be quite spectacular when seen in small telescopes and even in 10 × binoculars mounted on a tripod. The angular diameter of the disc varies between approximately 11 arc seconds and 60 arc seconds, and is 25 arc seconds when the phase is 50%. Maximum brightness occurs about 35 days before inferior conjunction (the passage of Venus between the Sun and the Earth), and under the most favourable conditions, which occur about every 8 years, can reach mag -4.4. Around maximum brightness, Venus is even visible in the daytime sky.

Venus can also transit the Sun, but these events are much rarer than transits of Mercury. They can only take place within a few days of 7 June and 8 December and occur in pairs separated by 8 years (or five synodic periods).

Thick clouds of sulphuric acid cover Venus making it impossible to see any surface features. Both Soviet and American probes have landed on Venus. (NASA/National Space Science Data Center (NSSDC))

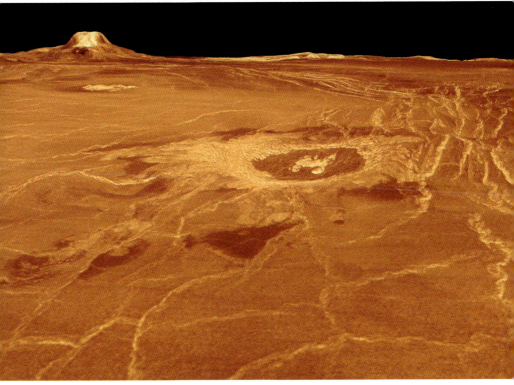

This image of the surface of Venus was computer-generated using radar data from the Magellan probe. Here you can see volcanoes rising from an arid plain. (NASA/NSSDC)

These transit pairs occur every 105.5 and 121.5 years, the last two events taking place in December 1874 and 1882, and the current pair occurring on 8 June 2004 and 6 June 2012. The 2012 event cannot be seen from southern Africa. The best places to view it are eastern Australia, New Zealand, Asia, Alaska and Hawaii.

Venus is almost a twin of the Earth in size and mass, and radar observations reveal that it spins on its own axis once every 243 days, in a retrograde direction (counter to the direction of its orbit). Thus a day on Venus lasts longer than the orbital period of 224.7 days. The surface of Venus cannot be seen, because it is continuously covered in clouds made of carbon dioxide and poisonous sulphuric acid. The atmosphere is very dense, 90 times the pressure of the air on Earth, and is much too hot to support any form of life. The temperature remains very high (over 475 °C) because the clouds keep the heat in, a phenomenon known as the 'greenhouse effect'. The winds on Venus are rather slow (a few kilometres per hour), but in the very dense atmosphere they have tremendous force, causing rapid erosion. Radar mapping reveals a surface of rolling plains, two high areas of land, and volcanoes that are probably active.

⊕ Earth

The Earth is the third planet from the Sun at a distance of 149 597 870 km, or one astronomical unit (AU). The polar axis is inclined at 23°27′ to the orbital plane and, as the planet spins, everything in the sky appears to rise and set in arcs of a circle.

The rotation of the Earth on its own axis causes the stars to appear to move through 15° in 1 hour, or 360° each day. During the course of a day the Earth moves along its orbital path by approximately 1°, and this causes a star that was on, say, the north–south line at a given time to reach the same position 3 minutes, 56 seconds earlier the following night.

Observations from Earth are severely hampered by the atmosphere. If you look over a car roof on a hot summer's day, the view appears turbulent because of the rising warm air. The same thing happens in the atmosphere at night, which gives the impression that the stars are twinkling. Objects are best observed when they are high in the sky, because their light travels a shorter distance through the Earth's atmosphere. Professional observatories are located on the tops of tall mountains to reduce the amount of atmospheric turbulence, and a few professional telescopes are equipped with computer-controlled 'active optics' that compensate for the distortions introduced by the atmosphere. However, the atmosphere blocks many wavelengths (which is a good thing for life on Earth) and so observations in the ultraviolet, X-ray and other wavelengths must be made from spacecraft. Optical observations are now also made from orbiting telescopes, the Hubble Space Telescope being the best-known example. Its successor, the James Webb Space Telescope (JWST), has an array of beryllium mirrors to observe only in the infrared spectrum. Its collecting mirror is almost six times as large as Hubble's. Unlike Hubble, which was in low-Earth orbit (150 km away), the JWST is designed to orbit 150 million km from Earth at the L2 Lagrangian point opposite the Sun, a Lagrange point being one of five possible places where a third body (like a satellite) can sit stationary with respect to two larger bodies (like the

This spectacular view of Earth was obtained by the Apollo 17 astronauts on their way to the Moon on 7 December 1972. It was the first time that the trajectory of an Apollo mission enabled a view of the south pole. Almost the entire coastline of Africa is visible, together with the Arabian Peninsula and the large island of Madagascar. The Earth's atmosphere is a very thin layer relative to its diameter. (NASA)

Earth and the Sun) that are orbiting each other because of gravity.

The Earth is the only planet that lies near the centre of the ecosphere, the volume of space around the Sun where conditions are suitable for life to exist. Venus is close to the inner limit but has a hot poisonous atmosphere, while Mars is too cold and its atmosphere is tenuous. The Earth is approximately 4.5 billion years old, and life appeared on its surface within the first billion years. Although the life on Earth is apparently unique in the solar system, most astronomers believe that there must be more inhabited planets around stars in our own and other galaxies. Several hundred extrasolar planets, or exoplanets, have been detected since 1995, including a few that could plausibly support life.

The future of life on our planet may be limited by a number of factors. As the Sun ages, its luminosity will gradually increase (at a rate of about 10% every 1.1 billion years) and this will cause carbon dioxide levels on Earth to increase to the point where plant life can no longer survive. The loss of plants will in turn lead to the rapid extinction of animals. If we manage to overcome the shorter-term threat posed by pollution, then the Earth is expected to remain habitable for another 500 million years.

The Earth itself has a longer, but still finite, future. As the Sun becomes more luminous and enters its red giant phase, its radius will expand until, about 4.5 billion years from now, it engulfs the Earth's present orbit. However, Earth's orbit is likely to have changed in the interim, and there are competing theories about what will happen. One theory suggests that the Sun's loss of mass will cause the radius of Earth's orbit to increase to about 1.7 AU, so that it escapes the expanding solar furnace; another says that tidal effects will cause Earth's orbit to decay so that it gradually spirals into the star, and thus precipitates its own demise. We can safely assume that neither event will be witnessed by any Earth-bound life forms.

Ultimately, in about another 5 billion years, the Sun will eject a planetary nebula and become a white dwarf.

Hubble made optical observations in low-Earth orbit. (Space Telescope Science Institute (STScI))

The James Webb Space Telescope will observe only in the infrared spectrum. (NASA)

THE MOON

Earth has only one natural satellite, the Moon, and the Earth–Moon system can be regarded as a binary pair. The ratio of the size of the satellite to that of the planet is greater than that of any other pair in the solar system except Pluto–Charon. The Moon is a nuisance to astronomers as its light interferes with observations for half of the month. In the future, astronomers may place an observatory on the Moon, which has no atmosphere and no pollution. The Moon always presents the same face to Earth, so a lunar day is equal to the time the Moon takes to revolve once around the Earth. If a telescope were to be placed on the far side of the Moon, so that the Earth could never be seen, there would be two weeks of total darkness followed by two weeks of total daylight. However, the lack of an atmosphere on the Moon means that the stars are still visible during the fortnight of daylight.

The Moon is the only other celestial body on which humankind has set foot. Indeed, since manned lunar exploration, lunar astronomy has largely ceased except for a few specialised observations such as laser-ranging. However, the Moon can be a rewarding object for study with binoculars or a small telescope, and it is also the easiest object to photograph.

Until recently, the Moon was thought to be dry. However in October 2009 NASA crashed both a two-ton rocket and the Lunar Crater Observation and Sensing Satellite (LCROSS) into the permanently shadowed Cebeus crater at the Moon's south pole. The impact threw up at least 100 litres of water and ice, which raises the possibility of using the Moon as a base for space exploration: the water could help sustain astronauts and provide raw material for rocket fuel. The Moon presents a disc 0.5° in diameter when viewed from Earth, and moves eastwards by this amount in 1 hour, so that it rises about 45 minutes later each day. New Moon occurs when it passes the Sun on its eastward path, and as it moves away from the Sun its disc becomes more illuminated until finally Full Moon occurs, when it is opposite the Sun and rises at sunset. As it again gets closer to the Sun, rising later each night, the phase decreases until New Moon is reached once again. The synodic period or interval between successive phases of Full Moon is 29 days, 12 hours, 44.03 minutes.

Near Full Moon, the moonscape is dominated by a number of very bright impact craters with lines of fracture radiating from them. The most dominant crater is Tycho, located in the southern lunar highlands (top of image) whose fracture lines are over 1 500 km long. This crater is very young, around 108 million years, based on the analysis of ray rocks collected during the Apollo 17 mission. The crater is sharply defined, unlike older craters that have suffered later impacts. (P. Mack)

Full Moon is not the best time to observe the Moon, because then there is very little contrast, although some of the brighter craters, such as Tycho, have brilliant rays emanating from them. The best contrast lies along 'the terminator', the boundary between day and night, and here the Sun casts long shadows during lunar sunrise (waxing Moon) or lunar sunset (waning Moon). When the Moon is only a few days from New and exhibits a thin crescent, a portion of the disc that is in lunar night is illuminated by light reflected from the Earth, a phenomenon called 'earthshine'.

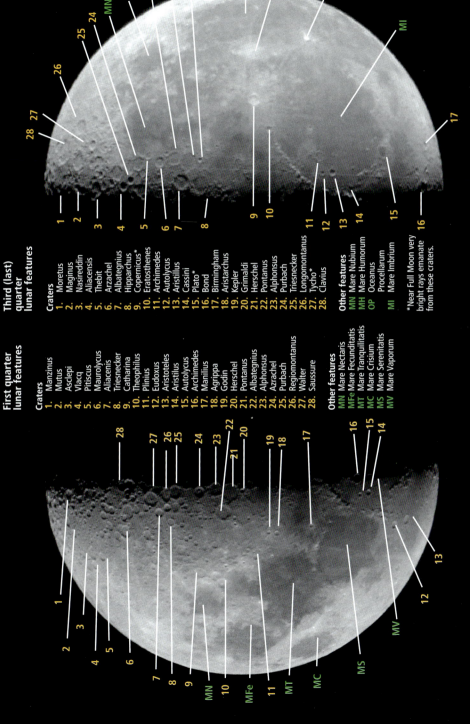

ECLIPSES

The Sun and the Moon follow roughly the same path in the sky, along the ecliptic, but the Moon completes one circuit in 27.3 days, while the Sun takes 365.25 days. When the Sun, Earth and Moon move into a straight line, an eclipse can occur. The planets also follow the path of the ecliptic and the Moon can pass in front of them and the background stars, causing a similar event called an 'occultation'.

There are two types of eclipse: lunar and solar, which occur only at Full and New Moon respectively. When sunlight falls on the Earth or the Moon it casts a long conical shadow within which the Sun cannot be seen. When one body moves into the shadow cone cast by the other an eclipse occurs. The shadow is made up of two regions, an 'umbra' and a 'penumbra'. The umbra is the cone that is in total shadow, while in the penumbral cone there is only partial shadow.

The umbral cone of the Earth varies in length as the distance between the Sun and the Earth changes, but it is always greater than three times the distance to the Moon. So if the Moon passes through this cone, a lunar eclipse must occur. The orbit of the Moon is inclined to the ecliptic and during most months it passes north or south of the shadow cone. When lunar eclipses do occur, they can be 'penumbral', 'partial' or 'total' depending on the depth of penetration into the shadow cone. The maximum duration of a lunar eclipse is 3 hours, 48 minutes, with totality accounting for 1 hour, 42 minutes. The Moon does not vanish completely during totality, because light is refracted through the Earth's atmosphere and falls onto the Moon, turning it reddish. The brightness of the Moon during totality depends on the amount of cloud and dust in the atmosphere. For example, dust in the upper atmosphere after a volcanic explosion can cause the eclipse to be dark copper-red. Total lunar eclipses are visible from a given point on Earth about every 3 years.

Solar eclipses are more spectacular, but rarer. The umbral shadow cone cast by the Moon is much smaller than that cast by the Earth, simply because the Moon is a relatively small body. On average the umbral cone extends 375 000 km, which is slightly less than the average Earth–Moon distance of 384 400 km. So under average conditions the Moon's umbral cone fails to

Different types of eclipses (not to scale):
a) A total eclipse of the Sun always occurs at New Moon. A total eclipse can be seen along a narrow track on the Earth's surface, while on either side a partial eclipse occurs.
b) An annular eclipse of the Sun, during which the Moon is further away from the Earth and the umbral cone fails to reach the surface. The Moon appears smaller than the Sun and the Sun's rim surrounds the lunar disc for an observer at the centre of the cone geometry.
c) A lunar eclipse always occurs at Full Moon and progresses from (1) penumbral to (2) partial to (3) total eclipse, when the Moon is entirely immersed in the Earth's umbral shadow. The sequence is mirrored as the Moon leaves the shadow cone (4, 5).

The photosphere and red prominences are visible in a total eclipse. (K. Kilburn)

A longer exposure reveals the corona. During an eclipse the sky darkens and stars are visible. (K. Kilburn)

The 'diamond ring' occurs at the onset and end of totality. The Sun's rays pour between the valleys of mountains on the lunar disc.
(S. Hodgkinson)

During a total annular eclipse the Moon is not large enough to block out all of the Sun and the result is a very bright ring with no corona. (P. Mack)

reach the surface of the Earth. Under such circumstances the angular diameter of the Moon appears slightly less than that of the Sun and if the three bodies line up an annular eclipse (from *annulus* meaning 'ring') occurs for places located in the centre of the cone geometry. Here the Sun appears to surround the rim of the Moon, an event that lasts for a maximum of 12 minutes, 24 seconds. Even on the cone axis the 'corona' (the Sun's outer atmosphere) cannot be seen because too much sunlight pours around the edges of the lunar disc, and at locations off the cone axis a partial eclipse occurs.

However, the Earth–Sun and the Earth–Moon distances vary slightly in accordance with Kepler's laws, and when the Earth is further away from the Sun than average, or the Moon is closer to the Earth than average, the Moon's umbral cone can reach the surface of the Earth. Under favourable circumstances, when both conditions are met, the cone can extend 29 300 km past the Earth and the dark track cast onto the Earth is 269 km wide. For an observer located within this region on Earth a total eclipse occurs, and for about 3 000 km on either side, a partial eclipse can be observed. Total eclipses of the Sun are very rare for a given point on Earth, and occur once every 360 years on average, while partial solar eclipses occur approximately every 6 years. The duration of totality depends on the latitude of the observer, and is longer at the equator, but it can never exceed 7 minutes, 40 seconds. In most cases it is much shorter. The lunar mountains cause the edge of the Moon's limb (circumference) to be ragged and, just before and after totality, the Sun's light spills between the mountains causing an effect known as 'Baily's beads', after the astronomer who first noticed them in the eclipse of 1836. Under certain circumstances the last glimpse of the Sun can give the appearance of a diamond ring.

A minimum of two solar eclipses must occur each year. The maximum possible number of eclipses per year is seven (four solar and three lunar, or five solar and two lunar), which last occurred in 1982. The next total solar eclipse over the southern part of Africa occurs on 25 November 2030. The only practical way to observe total eclipses is to travel to the eclipse path. Complete details can be found at Nasa's eclipse web site:
http://eclipse.gsfc.nasa.gov/eclipse.html

♂ Mars

Mars is the distinctive red planet situated fourth from the Sun at a mean distance of 1.52 AU. The orbit of Mars is very eccentric (0.093), more so than for any other planet except Mercury. A result of this is that the seasons are far more extreme in its southern hemisphere, which has its summer near perihelion (the point of closest approach to the Sun), and its winter near aphelion (the point of greatest distance from the Sun), than in the northern hemisphere, where the opposite applies. The synodic period (interval between closest approaches to Earth) is greater than that of any other planet because of the relative motion of Mars with respect to the Earth. The value

This composite image shows Mars's Valles Marineris hemisphere. The canyon shown is more than 3 000 km long and as much as 8 km in depth. To the north, ancient river channels are visible. They end in the Acidalia Planitia basin, visible at the top of the image. The three dark red spots in the west are Tharsis volcanoes, about 25 km in diameter. Many impact craters pock the ancient area south of the Valles Marineris canyon. (NASA/NSSDC)

In 1980 the Viking Orbiter took the 100 images that comprise this picture of Mars's Syrtis Major hemisphere. At the top left of the photograph is the bright area Arabia. At the right is a volcanic ridge, Syrtis Major Planus, which looks darker. A cap of carbon dioxide frost can be seen at the south pole. (NASA/NSSDC)

varies slightly depending on the distance of Mars from the Sun, but on average is 780 days. As a consequence, Mars only disappears from view every other year, but then remains invisible for a longer period than any other planet, usually several months.

The distance of Mars from the Earth varies between 0.36 and 2.64 AU, and so the brightness of the planet changes considerably, reaching mag -2.8 under the most favourable circumstances. This always occurs around August at intervals of 15 and 17 years, when Mars is in the southern part of the ecliptic, and so southern Africa is one of the best observing sites. The next highly favourable opposition will occur in July 2018.

However, Mars is a rather unrewarding planet to study with small telescopes as it reveals very little detail. It is slightly more than half the diameter of the Earth and rotates on its own axis once every 24 hours, 37 minutes, presenting a very slightly different face each night. Mars also has seasons very similar to those on the Earth, except that they are much longer because a Martian year lasts 687 days. The surface is very rocky, covered in reddish dust, and has frozen water and carbon dioxide beneath the soil. The Martian atmosphere is very thin, but strong turbulent winds occasionally cause global dust storms similar to those occurring in the deserts on Earth. Mars is also cratered and has very large canyons and volcanoes. The most notable features to the telescopic observer are the polar caps, which consist of frozen carbon dioxide. Other features include the dark areas like Syrtis Major, which were once thought to be canals dug out by Martians. Not visible with Earth-based telescopes is the gigantic volcano Nix Olympica, some 480 km in diameter and three times as high as Mount Everest.

Mars has two small satellites, Phobos and Deimos, discovered in August 1877 by Asaph Hall using a 660 mm refractor, the largest of its type at the time. Phobos

In January 2004 NASA landed the rovers Spirit and Opportunity on the surface of Mars. Although only intended to last for 90 days, they lasted for 5 years. The geological samples they took proved that, at some point, Mars was a wet planet. (NASA/JPL/Cornell University)

and Deimos are irregularly shaped, about 30 km in size and in very close orbit to the planet. They are probably captured asteroids. Too small to light up the Martian sky at night, they can only be seen with large telescopes.

Because Mars is the closest planet to Earth it is a natural destination for unmanned probes – almost 50 have been launched. NASA's Mars exploration rovers, Spirit and Opportunity, landed on the surface in January 2004 for a planned mission of 90 'sols', or Martian days. These robots proved to be highly successful. The first rover to stop working was Spirit – after 2 210 sols, or more than 24 times its expected lifetime. Mars will be the first planet targeted for manned exploration, probably within the next 20 years.

♃ Jupiter

The outer four planets are called the 'gas giants' because of their sheer size (compared to the terrestrial planets) and composition. Jupiter is the largest planet in the solar system. At 1/1 000th the mass of the Sun it is more than twice as massive and more voluminous than all the other planets put together. Jupiter thus has a very strong gravitational field and even the lightest of elements, hydrogen, has not escaped from its surface. Its gravitational pull can disturb minor members of the solar system such as comets. Unlike the planets closer to the Sun, Jupiter has no solid surface but is a largely liquid body (90% hydrogen, 10% helium and traces of methane, water and ammonia) with a possible rocky core surrounded by layers of liquid hydrogen and, ultimately, a thin gaseous atmosphere. Thus we effectively look at cloud tops rather than a fixed surface. These clouds are extremely cold, around -150 °C. The composition of Jupiter, and especially of its core, is controversial, but the Juno mission (launched in August 2011) may clarify this. Jupiter gives out more energy than it receives from the Sun; the excess is thought to be generated by the slight contraction of the planet under its own gravity.

Despite its size, Jupiter spins on its own axis in less than 10 hours. Such rapid rotation, combined with its size and lack of solidity, results in its being appreciably oblate: it bulges at the equator. The equatorial diameter is 142 984 km and the polar diameter is 133 708 km. Jupiter is the fifth planet out from the Sun at a distance of 5.2 AU (778 570 000 km) and so it takes 11.86 Earth years to orbit the Sun or make one complete circuit of the ecliptic.

To date this is the most highly detailed image of the gas giant Jupiter. It is a composite of four photographs taken from the Cassini spacecraft during its close approach to the planet in December 2000. The Great Red Spot is a vortex that can be seen from Earth even with an amateur's telescope. The black dot is a shadow cast by the moon Europa. (NASA)

The synodic period is 399 days, so oppositions occur about a month later each year. Perihelion oppositions (when the Sun, Earth and Jupiter are aligned, and Jupiter's orbit has brought it as close to Earth as possible) occur about every 12 years, in September or October. The first of these this century was on 21 September 2010 when the diameter of the disc was 49.8 arc seconds. However, all oppositions are well worth watching. The planet cannot be seen for about 6 to 8 weeks each year when it is too closely aligned to the Sun for telescopic study. At its brightest it dominates the night sky at mag -2.9. At all times it is brighter than mag -1.6, or any star in the sky. The

Earth overtakes Jupiter every 399 days as it orbits the Sun and, as it does so, Jupiter appears to undergo retrograde motion, travelling backwards against the background stars. Each successive opposition occurs about 30° east of the previous one. This corresponds to the 12 zodiacal constellations and may have been the historical origin of the signs.

Observationally, Jupiter is the most rewarding planet, even when using a small amateur telescope or binoculars. Its surface is dominated by a series of belts that are confined to different latitudes. The two most prominent ones are at low latitudes and are known as the 'equatorial belts'. The south equatorial belt has two components, the more southerly of which contains the famous Great Red Spot, an enormous eddy and the longest surviving feature in Jupiter's atmosphere. This feature, which is visible in a modest telescope, reveals the rapid rotation of the planet. To get some idea of the sheer size of Jupiter, imagine the Earth as an apple: if you peeled its skin and laid it out, it would just cover the area of the Great Red Spot.

Jupiter has at least 64 named natural satellites, most under 10 km in diameter and discovered since 1975 by visiting spacecraft. Only four of them are visible using small instruments. They are the Galilean moons Io, Europa, Ganymede and Callisto, and they are easily seen with binoculars. These moons are named after Galileo Galilei, who, 400 years ago and using one of the first telescopes ever built, was the first person to see them. They all lie in the equatorial plane of the planet, which is tilted at 3° to the orbital plane. This small angle of inclination means that the satellites undergo occultations and eclipses by the planet and can transit the Jovian disc. For a few months every 5 or 6 years the satellites can also occult each other, and observations of such events provide accurate orbital information. Jupiter and its moons were extensively investigated over an 8-year period by the Galileo spacecraft. At the mission's end in 2003, the vehicle was deliberately crashed into the Jovian atmosphere, to avoid any possibility of contaminating the moons with bacteria from Earth. Among many other discoveries, it found strong evidence of liquid water below the surfaces of Europa, Ganymede and Callisto. In Europa's case there may well be entire oceans trapped under the moon's icy

At 4 821 km in diamater, Callisto is the third largest satellite in the solar system – only Neptune's Titan and another Jovian moon, Ganymede, are larger. Callisto orbits at a greater distance from Jupiter than do Io, Europa and Ganymede. Its surface is marked by ancient craters that date back about 3.8 billion years and it shows no signs of resurfacing. This suggests that it lacks a separate core, mantle and crust, which would undergo tectonic or volcanic processes. The atmosphere is thin and comprises mainly carbon dioxide. (NASA/JPL)

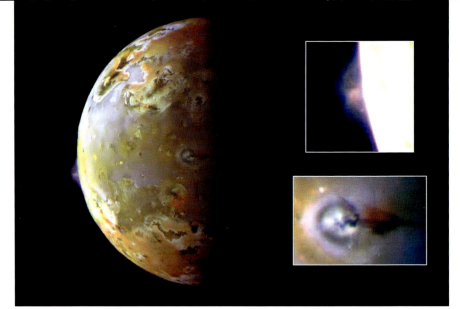

Jupiter exerts immense tidal forces on Io, causing volcanic activity: Io is one of the most geologically active bodies in our solar system. This image, taken by the robotic Galileo spacecraft, which orbited Jupiter between 1995 and 2003, shows two erupting sulphur volcanoes. The first plume is clearly visible at the limb, rising 140 km above the Pilan Patera crater (inset top). The second eruption, near the centre of the image, rises about 75 km above the surface, casting a shadow (inset bottom). This ring-shaped plume is named for Prometheus who, in Greek mythology, gave mortals fire. Prometheus is visible in every image taken of Io since the Voyager flybys of 1979, suggesting that this volcano is a long-term active feature. (Galileo Project/JPL/NASA)

surface. Another moon, Io, has volcanism 100 times greater than Earth's, and also exhibits enormous electrical activity in its atmosphere. The Europa Jupiter System Mission, planned for 2020, will be a joint NASA/European Space Agency (ESA) venture to explore Europa, Ganymede, and the magnetosphere of Jupiter. Jupiter has a ring system similar to that around Saturn, but it is much more tenuous, and was apparently formed by dust ejected from the moons by impacting meteorites.

Ganymede is the largest satellite in the solar system with a diameter of 5 262 km. It is larger than Mercury, Pluto, and the Earth's moon. If Ganymede orbited the Sun instead of orbiting Jupiter it would easily be classified as a planet. Ganymede has undergone a complex geological history. Approximately 40% of the surface is covered by heavily cratered dark regions and the rest of the surface is covered by a light-coloured grooved terrain creating a complex pattern. This image was obtained by the Galileo spacecraft. (NASA/JPL)

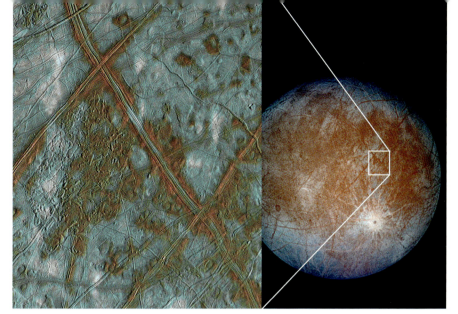

Europa's crust is made up of blocks that geologists believe have floated into new positions, transported by a subsurface ocean. The reddish-brown areas represent non-ice material resulting from geological activity. The prominent Pwyll impact crater has a series of white rays of ejected material. Icy plains are shown in blue tones. The long dark lines are ridges and fractures in the crust, some of which are more than 3 000 km long. This is a composite image obtained by the orbiting Galileo spacecraft from a distance of 670 000 km. (NASA/JPL/University of Arizona)

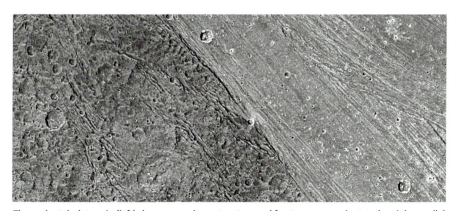

The ancient dark terrain (left) shows many impact craters and fracture zones orientated mainly parallel to the boundary between the dark and bright regions of Ganymede. In contrast, the bright terrain (right) is less cratered and relatively smooth. The image was taken in May 2000 from a distance of 11 800 km and shows an area approximately 213 by 97 km. (NASA/JPL/German Aerospace Centre (DLR))

We have noted that all of the planets lie in a flat disc or plane around the Sun's equator. The Galilean moons of Jupiter also lie within a disc, and their motion can be observed with a small pair of binoculars. These disc structures are very common in astronomical arrangements and, as we shall soon discuss, are present in galaxies.

♄ Saturn

Saturn is the second largest planet in the solar system and is located nearly twice as far away from the Sun as Jupiter, at 9.54 AU. Its sidereal period (the time taken to orbit the Sun) is 29.46 years and so Saturn moves very slowly eastwards along the ecliptic – it is usually visible for 10 months of the year. The planet spins on its axis once every 10 hours, 40.8 minutes, and the rotational axis is inclined to the orbital plane by 26.7°. This results in alternate poles being well presented to the Earth approximately every 15 years. Likewise, twice during each orbital period its famous rings are presented edge-on and disappear from view for a few days. This last occurred on 4 September 2009. At opposition, the disc of Saturn subtends between 14 arc seconds and 20 arc seconds, depending on the distance, and, like Jupiter, it is rather oblate. Saturn's synodic period is 378 days, and so successive oppositions occur about two weeks later each year. The observing

Artist's montage using images obtained by the Voyager 1 spacecraft in November 1980. Dione is in the foreground, followed in clockwise order by Enceladus, Rhea, Titan, Mimas and Tethys. (NASA/JPL)

conditions vary during the synodic period: for 14 years the planet lies in the northern hemisphere, reaching declination +26, then for the next 14 years it moves south and is well placed for southern hemisphere viewers. Since 2009 it has been moving south in the southern hemisphere, and it will reach its southernmost point in 2017.

Saturn is another largely liquid planet consisting of 75% liquid hydrogen and 25% liquid helium with traces of methane and ammonia and a small core of molten rocky material. It appears to possess a thicker atmosphere than Jupiter. Saturn's overall density of 0.7g·cm^{-3} is less than that of any other planet, and so it would, in theory, float on water. Saturn also has dark belts and light zones in its cloud tops that are very cold (-180 °C), but these are obscured by a thin hazy layer in the upper atmosphere.

Near-infrared image obtained by Hubble on 4 January 1998. The colours indicate atmospheric layers. Sunlight shining through the rings is projected onto the disc as a white band. Dione is at the lower left; Tethys is at the top right. (Erich Karkoschka, University of Arizona/NASA)

This composite of Hubble images shows how the view of Saturn's rings changed over a span of 7 years during the planet's 29-year orbit of the Sun. The bottom left image shows autumn in the northern hemisphere, the upper right image shows northern winter. (NASA/Hubble Heritage Team/STScI/Association of Universities for Research in Astronomy (AURA))

Saturn is famous for its ring system, but this is not unique in the solar system: Jupiter, Uranus and Neptune possess similar, though less impressive systems. The rings around Saturn are very prominent and can be split into six distinct streams, although the two Voyager spacecraft, flying by in 1980 and 1981 respectively, revealed even more complex divisions. The rings are less than 1 km thick and consist of millions of particles, which probably range in size from a tennis ball to a football. The rings are unstable and are probably just a few hundred million years old.

This planet gives out almost two-and-a-half times the amount of energy it receives from the Sun, an effect probably due to the gravitational separation of hydrogen and helium, and so, like Jupiter's, its core is probably hot.

Saturn has 62 known satellites, of which only 13 have a diameter greater than 50 km. The largest by far is Titan, which is 5 150 km in diameter, bigger than the planet Mercury. Titan is the only satellite in the solar system that retains a substantial atmosphere, composed chiefly of nitrogen and methane. Its surface is hidden by a reddish smog, but the Cassini spacecraft, which visited Saturn and Titan in 2004, and its companion Huygens vehicle, which actually landed on Titan, revealed lakes of liquid methane and networks of dry river beds (which must have been carved by liquid methane, as it is far too cold for water).

THE SOLAR SYSTEM   41

⛢ Uranus

The two outer planets, Uranus and Neptune, are much fainter than those we've discussed so far, and were only discovered after the invention of the telescope.

Uranus is approximately twice as far from the Sun as Saturn and 19 times as far away as the Earth. It takes 84 years to orbit the Sun, moving just 4.5° eastwards along the ecliptic each year. At opposition it is just visible to the naked eye at mag 5.7, but even a very large telescope reveals little detail, just a pale greenish disc only 4 arc seconds in diameter. The green hue is caused by the absorption of red light in the methane-rich atmosphere. Oppositions occur every 370 days, or about four days later each year. Uranus is currently just south of the equator in Pisces, moving very slowly northwards, with oppositions occurring in September.

Uranus was discovered in 1781 by William Herschel, then an unknown English amateur astronomer, using a home-made reflecting telescope.

Its spin axis is inclined at 98° to the ecliptic so it 'rolls on its side' in a retrograde manner. One day on Uranus lasts 17.24 hours.

Like the other gaseous planets, Uranus has numerous satellites and a ring system. The five largest satellites are named after characters in Shakespeare's *A Midsummer Night's Dream*. In order of increasing distance from the planet they are Miranda, Ariel, Umbriel, Titania and Oberon.

Uranus has a system of 13 extremely faint rings, which cannot be seen directly from Earth without specialist imaging techniques. The first nine were discovered from South Africa in 1977 by Joseph Churms and Pat Booth. They were detected when Uranus passed in front of a bright star, causing the starlight to be modulated. The rings reflect only a tiny fraction of the light falling on them – they are made of material much darker than coal dust. The Voyager 2 spacecraft passed Uranus on 26 January 1986 and obtained a spectacular series of photographs of the rings and the five previously known satellites, as well as discovering nine new satellites and two new rings. A further two rings were found in Hubble Space Telescope images between 2003 and 2005.

The rotation axis of Uranus is the most inclined of any planet and it appears to 'roll over' along its orbital path. This enhanced Hubble Space Telescope image shows the faint ring system, which is made of dust and small pebbles. The bright satellite at the lower right corner is Ariel. Five small satellites with dark surfaces can be seen just outside the ring system. Clockwise from the top they are Desdemona, Belinda, Portia, Cressida and Puck. (Erich Karkoschka, University of Arizona/NASA)

Neptune

Astronomers had observed that the orbital path of Uranus did not follow its predicted track, and in 1834 the Rev. T. Hussey, another English amateur astronomer, proposed that this could be explained by the presence of another planet further out. Two professional astronomers, Adams in England and Le Verrier in France, worked independently on the problem. Adams reported his results to the Astronomer Royal who did not take immediate action. In the meantime Galle and D'Arrest used Le Verrier's predictions and very quickly located the new planet, Neptune, on 23 September 1846. It was the first planet to be discovered by computation.

Neptune is about the same size as Uranus, or four times the diameter of Earth. It is an exceedingly remote, icy cold place (-228 °C), located some 30 AU

Launched in 1977 NASA's Voyager 2 spacecraft visited the four outer gas giant planets, taking 12 years at an average velocity of 19 km·s^{-1} to reach Neptune. These planets lack solid surfaces but have massive amounts of hydrogen and helium, with traces of other gases such as methane. (NASA, Voyager 2, Calvin J. Hamilton)

Mathematician Urbain Le Verrier (1811–1877) played a key role in the discovery of Neptune.

from the Sun. Like Jupiter and Saturn, it gives out more heat than it receives from the Sun. Neptune has a warm core and active weather systems, including major mobile storms and the strongest winds in the solar system, reaching 2 000 km·hr^{-1}. The atmosphere is 80% hydrogen, 19% helium, with trace amounts of methane. The methane absorbs red wavelengths so the planet appears bluish.

Neptune spins on its own axis once every 16 hours, 7 minutes and takes almost 165 years to orbit the Sun or go once around the ecliptic. At mag 7, the planet never reaches naked eye visibility, although it can be seen with binoculars. It is remarkable that Galileo, while observing Jupiter and its moons through his primitive telescope in 1612, happened

THE SOLAR SYSTEM

to record the position of Neptune, which he apparently mistook for a fixed star. Neptune's movement across the starry background is very slow. Because it is so far away, the planet appears less than 2.5 arc seconds in diameter and a powerful telescope is required to resolve it as a disc. Neptune is currently well placed for observation from southern Africa, as it is located in the constellation of Capricornus.

The planet was visited by the Voyager 2 spacecraft on 25 August 1989. Until then only two satellites had been known: Triton, still by far the largest of Neptune's satellites, with a diameter of 2 707 km, was discovered by Lassell in 1846, just 17 days after the discovery of Neptune itself. Triton moves in a retrograde orbit and is easily visible through a small telescope. Nereid, 340 km in diameter, is remarkable for its highly eccentric orbit, which takes it well outside Neptune's magnetic field.

Most of what we now know about Neptune was gleaned from the Voyager 2 encounter. Voyager 2 discovered six new satellites, named Proteus, Larissa, Despina, Galatea, Thalassa and Naiad. Another five were discovered between 2002 and 2003, bringing the current count of Neptunian moons to 13. All of these moons are very small, ranging in diameter from 50 km for Naiad to 1 180 km for Despina, and they have very low reflectivity, making them almost impossible to observe from Earth. They all lie inside Neptune's magnetic field. Some show signs of geological activity and impact craters. Based on observations of the brightness of partly occulted stars as the planet wandered across the

The Voyager 2 spacecraft imaged the very tenuous ring system of Neptune. All four gas giants have a ring system. To capture the very faint rings, a mask was used to block the bright light from the planet during the 591-second exposure. Three main rings are clearly visible. (NASA/JPL)

Voyager 2 passed within 40 000 km of Triton, which, with a diameter of 2 707 km, is the largest of Neptune's moons. It has a tenuous atmosphere that is very cold, at -235 °C. (NASA)

sky, astronomers had long suspected the presence of rings around the planet. Voyager 2 discovered six very narrow rings, composed of exceptionally dark material. They are discontinuous arcs and may be very unstable. Observations made from Earth in 2002 and 2003 already showed substantial changes from the Voyager 2 images. It is thought that some of the arcs may disappear in as little as a century.

One of the biggest surprises from Voyager 2 was the discovery of an atmosphere around Triton, albeit an extremely tenuous one, with only 10^{-4} times the density of Earth's atmosphere. It is composed of 99% nitrogen, with some traces of methane and carbon monoxide. Triton is also smaller and denser than previously thought, and probably consists of two-thirds rock and one-third ice.

Neptune was Voyager 2's last planetary rendezvous. By 2020 it will have passed through the Oort cometary cloud and will in effect have left the solar system. If the spacecraft survives, then hundreds of thousands of years from now it will travel beyond the nearest stars, by which time civilisation on Earth, as we know it, may well have ceased to exist.

This Voyager 2 image shows an area of Neptune's surface that is about 480 km across. A young crater sits in an older lava flow. (NASA/JPL)

THE SOLAR SYSTEM

DWARF PLANETS

Accurate measurements of the orbital motion of Neptune revealed some gravitational discrepancies, which naturally led to the prediction of a ninth planet.

Percival Lowell built an observatory in Flagstaff, Arizona, and in 1909 started searching for the elusive ninth planet, but he had no success. Many people tried looking during the period from 1913 to 1915, again without success. Ironically, Lowell died in 1916, never knowing that he had actually photographed the planet. The 'ninth planet' was eventually discovered in 1930 by Clyde Tombaugh at the Lowell Observatory.

For over 75 years Pluto was thought of as the ninth planet. This body's strange behaviour, and the subsequent discovery of an even more distant and massive object, has led astronomers to redefine the term 'planet' and create a new class of objects called 'dwarf planets'. Before we take a look at Pluto in some detail it is necessary to discuss this new definition.

The International Astronomical Union (IAU) has now defined three types of bodies, as follows:

A 'planet' is officially defined as a celestial body that (a) is in orbit around the Sun, (b) has sufficient mass for its self-gravity to overcome rigid body forces so that it assumes a hydrostatic equilibrium (a nearly spherical shape), and (c) has cleared the neighbourhood around its orbit.

A 'dwarf planet' satisfies conditions (a) and (b) but has failed condition (c) and in addition is not a satellite of another planet.

Almost 2 years after the IAU introduced the category of dwarf planets they decided to adopt the name 'plutoid' for trans-Neptunian dwarf planets similar to Pluto. Plutoids have highly elliptical orbits and lie at an average distance beyond the orbit of Neptune. Satellites of plutoids are not themselves plutoids, even if they are so massive that their shape is dictated by self-gravity.

We now know of thousands of trans-Neptunian objects that are not dwarf planets. This region of the solar system is known as the 'Kuiper Belt'.

There are presently five known dwarf planets, and their best current measurements are indicated in the table below.

Name	Plutoid?	Discovery date	Mean distance from Sun (AU)	Orbital period (years)	Orbital inclination (°)	Diameter (km)	Mass (Earth = 1)	Satellites
Ceres	No	1801	2.77	4.60	9.73	975	0.00015	0
Pluto	Yes	1930	39.44	248	17.1	2 320	0.00218	4
Makemake	Yes	2005	45.79	310	29.0	~1 600	0.0005	0
Haumea	Yes	2004	43.13	283	28.2	1 960 x 1 518 x 996	0.0007	2
Eris	Yes	2005	67.67	557	44.187	2 400	0.0028	1

Data for the five known dwarf planets. With the exception of Ceres (discovered in 1801) and Pluto, all of the data should be considered preliminary.

Pluto

Pluto has a very eccentric orbit that is inclined at an angle of 17.1° to the ecliptic. At perihelion its distance from the Sun is 4.5×10^9 km (30 AU), bringing it inside the orbit of Neptune, while at aphelion it is 7.5×10^9 km (49 AU). Pluto is thus exceedingly remote, approximately 40 times further away from the Sun than is the Earth, and receives virtually no heat. It is an icy object with a temperature of -230 °C. The orbital period of Pluto is almost 248 Earth years. When it passed perihelion in 1989, it attained only mag 14.9, requiring a telescope with an aperture of at least 350 mm to see it.

A small telescope will not show this planet as a disc; only its motion across the background stars will portray its true nature. The diameter of Pluto is somewhat uncertain, but it is very small. Latest estimates suggest it is no more than 2 320 km, or one-fifth of Earth's diameter. Pluto has four known satellites. The largest, at 1 207 km, is Charon, discovered at the Lowell Observatory in 1978. The orbital

Although New Horizons was the fastest spacecraft ever launched, achieving lunar orbit in just 9 hours, it was still expected to take 13 months to reach Jupiter and over 9 years to reach Pluto, in 2015. (NASA)

period is 6.387 days. Pluto and Charon entered a 5-year period of mutual eclipses between 1985 and 1990. This occurs when the Pluto–Charon orbital plane is edge-on as seen from Earth, an event that only happens twice in Pluto's 248-year orbital period. By observing these eclipses it was possible to take spectra of Pluto alone and then of the pair. The results show that Charon is a large icy body dominated by water, whereas Pluto is covered with nitrogen and methane. The mass ratio of Pluto–Charon is greater than for any other solar system pair, including the Earth–Moon. Charon is 11.6% the mass of Pluto, while the Moon is only 1.2% the mass of Earth. Pluto's remaining moons, Hydra, Nix and P4 (preliminary), are very small.

NASA's New Horizons spacecraft was launched in January 2006, flew past Jupiter in 2007 and is due to reach Pluto in July 2015. Having travelled some 5 billion km it must pass through a circle only 300 km across to achieve its scientific goals. It has imaging cameras and a dust collector called Venetia, after the 11-year-old girl who named the then-ninth planet when it was discovered in 1930.

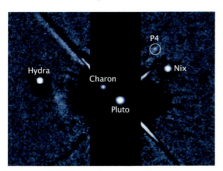

Pluto was discovered in 1930 and was long considered to be the ninth planet. The recent discovery of similar distant objects even further away, however, has led to Pluto being reclassified as a dwarf planet. Pluto has one major moon called Charon and three smaller moons called Nix, Hydra and P4 (upon discovery in June 2011). (NASA, ESA and M. Showalter (SETI))

THE SOLAR SYSTEM 47

Eris

The largest dwarf planet was discovered in 2005 by Mike Brown, Chad Trujillo and David Rabinowitz in an ongoing survey at the Palomar Observatory. When they announced the discovery in 2005 they provisionally named it 2003 UB313. In 2006 they suggested the name Eris – the goddess of war and strife in Greek mythology. She stirs up jealousy and envy, causing fighting and anger among men. Eris certainly stirred up a great deal of trouble at the IAU meeting in Prague. By the end of the conference members had voted to demote Pluto and Eris to dwarf planet status, leaving the solar system with only eight planets.

Eris has one satellite, called Dysnomia, Eris's daughter in Greek mythology and the spirit of lawlessness. These two objects are the most distant ever seen in the solar system, at 67.67 AU.

Haumea

This is another dwarf planet and was discovered in 2004, also by Mike Brown's team. The discovery of Haumea was again surrounded by controversy, as a Spanish team accessed Brown's observation logs, which provided enough information for them to locate the object on plates they had taken earlier for a different purpose. They then tried to take credit for the

Haumea and its moons. Haumea is at the centre with Hi'iaka above it and Namaka directly below it. (NASA)

Eris is both the most massive known dwarf planet, being 27% larger than Pluto, and the one that is furthest from us. It orbits the Sun at approximately 100 AU, making it three times more distant than Pluto, together with its moon Dysnomia. The orbital period is 557 years. This image was obtained by the Hubble Space Telescope in July 2007. (NASA/ESA/M. Brown)

An artist's impression of Haumea and its two moons. This dwarf planet measures approximately 1 960 x 1 518 x 996 km. (NASA/StScI)

discovery. It is named after a Hawaiian goddess in recognition of the location of the discovering telescope on Mauna Kea. With an orbital period of 283 years and mag 17.3, this is the third brightest object in the Kuiper Belt and is easily visible with a large amateur telescope. The brightness of Haumea varies significantly over a period of 3.9 hours, and it is thought to be an ellipsoid body: although it is believed to be in hydrostatic equilibrium (permitting its classification as a dwarf planet), its rapid rotation is causing it to deform from a spherical to an ellipsoidal shape. Haumea has a very reflective surface (similar to water ice) and has a dark reddish spot, possibly an impact feature. This information will no doubt evolve as more observations are made. Two small satellites orbit Haumea – Hi'iaka and Namaka.

Makemake

Another dwarf planet discovered by Mike Brown's team is Makemake, found in 2005. Makemake (pronounced 'MAH-kay-MAH-kay') is the third largest known dwarf planet in the solar system. It is roughly three-quarters the size of Pluto and orbits at a distance of 52 AU, with a period of 310 years. It will be at opposition in 2033. Uniquely among the plutoids, it has no satellites. The average temperature there is -243.2 °C, which is exceedingly low. The surface is probably covered with methane, ethane and nitrogen ices.

Makemake as imaged by an amateur telescope in November 2009. (K. Heider)

An artist's impression of Makemake. This dwarf planet may or may not be spherical. (NASA/StScI)

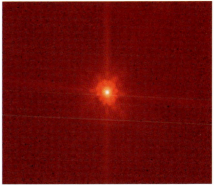

Makemake as imaged by the Hubble Space Telescope in November 2006. (NASA)

CERES AND THE ASTEROID BELT

Ceres is the smallest dwarf planet in the solar system, and the only one that is not a plutoid, orbiting the Sun at a distance of 2.77 AU between the orbits of Mars and Jupiter. It is almost certain that no other non-plutoid dwarf planet will be discovered.

Mathematically there appeared to be a missing body between the orbits of Mars and Jupiter, so in 1800 a group of six astronomers formulated a joint plan to search for it. Before they put their ideas into action the object was accidentally discovered on 1 January 1801, by Giuseppe Piazzi.

This tiny body, only 975 km in diameter, was named Ceres. By itself it was too small to satisfy the mathematics, and so the search continued. Pallas, Juno and Vesta were discovered in the following 6 years, but the planet hunters disbanded when no more discoveries

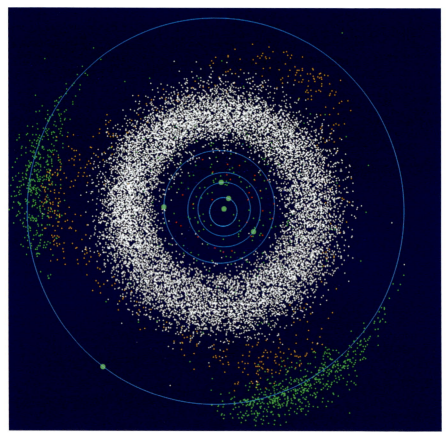

A plot of all known asteroids positioned for August 2006. The central green dot is the Sun and (moving outwards in order) the blue circles show the orbits of Mercury, Venus, Earth, Mars and Jupiter. The main asteroid belt is shown in white. The 'Greek' and 'Trojan' asteroids (green) are trapped at two Lagrangian points in Jupiter's orbit. The 'Hildas' (orange) are just inside the orbit of Jupiter.

were forthcoming. However, a fifth minor planet, Astraea, was discovered in 1845. Since 1948, not a single year has passed without there being at least one discovery, and currently hundreds are discovered (i.e. their orbits are exactly determined) each year.

With the exception of Ceres, which is classified as a dwarf planet, all of these other objects are called 'asteroids' or 'small solar system bodies'. The term 'minor planet' is now defunct.

Recent estimates suggest that there are probably over 1.2 million asteroids larger than 1 km in the main belt. Some of the asteroids can reach naked eye visibility, and many are visible with binoculars. No details can be seen because of their very small size. Vesta is the brightest at mag 6, just at the limit of naked eye detection. Most of the modern discoveries are made by accident on routine survey images taken for other purposes. The images are exposed for several hours and, during this time, the telescope tracks the stars very precisely. The asteroids show up as trails, because they have moved against the starry background during the exposure. The smallest objects are less than a few hundred metres in diameter and are often very irregular in shape. Unlike the planets, which are confined to the plane of the ecliptic, asteroids can have highly inclined orbits. Their origin is still rather uncertain, but they may be the remains of a planet or planets destroyed early on in the formation of the solar system, perhaps shattered by a close encounter with another object.

The Dawn mission was launched in September 2007 and was projected to visit Vesta in 2011/2012, followed by Ceres in 2015. Dawn will investigate Vesta's magnetism in the hope of shedding light on the mechanisms of geomagnetism on Earth, Mars and Mercury, while the probe will search for water and possibly a thin atmosphere on Ceres.

Many advanced amateur astronomers play key roles in discovering and measuring the orbits of small solar system bodies. One particular class, called 'near-Earth objects' or NEOs, are of public interest because of the possibility of collision with Earth.

COMETS

The unexpected appearance of a bright comet in the sky has always excited observers. Even today comets remain the most unpredictable members of the solar system. While the planets move in nearly circular paths around the Sun, comets have very eccentric orbits, often at high inclinations to the ecliptic. Comets fall into two distinct groups depending on their orbital periods.

Halley's Comet, during the 1985/86 apparition, as seen from South Africa. (P. Mack)

First, we know of just over 100 'short-period' comets (with return times of less than a few hundred years), which are contained within the realm of the planets and have fairly predictable orbits. They tend to be very faint and are not normally visible in amateur equipment. The exception is Halley's Comet, which is the only bright comet with an orbital period of less than several centuries. It last returned in 1986 and will reach perihelion again in 2062. Our knowledge of Halley's Comet was dramatically increased in March 1986 when the European Giotto and Russian Vega spacecraft obtained close-up images of the nucleus.

The second class comprises the 'long-period' comets, which are far brighter and more numerous. Their orbits are extremely eccentric and can reach out far beyond the orbit of the planets, perhaps even a quarter of the way to the nearest stars, and they take thousands or even millions of years to complete a single orbit.

Comets consist of three basic parts: a nucleus, a coma and a tail. The heart of the comet is the nucleus, which is like a dirty black ice-ball, as dark as coal dust, and about 10 km in diameter. The nucleus of Comet Halley is potato-shaped and measures 14×8 km. The coma develops as ice in the nucleus sublimates, forming a mini atmosphere around the nucleus as the comet approaches the Sun. A tail can develop, often split into two branches – one containing gas and the other dust. This can stretch out to several million kilometres and always points away from the Sun. The Deep Impact mission in July 2005 successfully collided an impactor spacecraft with the nucleus of Comet 9P/Tempel. Flyby images taken by the 'mother ship' revealed a large cloud of bright dust, suggesting that the nucleus contains more dust and less ice than previously believed.

The Stardust mission (2004–2006) actually returned with samples from the coma of Comet Wild 2, and the spacecraft

Comet McNaught 2006 P1 was the brightest comet to be seen from southern Africa in nearly 40 years. The blue ionised gas in the tail is pushed away by the solar wind. (Dr Steve Potter)

has now been reassigned to collect more images of the artificial crater on 9P/Tempel.

Comets are thought to come from a vast reservoir known as the 'Oort Cloud' (named after the astronomer who first thought of the idea) situated about 60 000 AU from the Sun, at the very edge of the solar system.

METEORS

Meteors are the smallest members of the solar system, so small, in fact, that they cannot be seen outside the Earth's atmosphere. They typically range in size from a speck of dust to the size of a small house, although the larger meteors are much rarer, and the majority seen by the unaided eye are less than the size of a small coin. Some 20 million tiny meteors enter the Earth's atmosphere each day, but they are nearly always destroyed in the upper atmosphere, which they enter at a speed typically between 35 and 95 km·s^{-1}. The air resistance quickly heats the particle to incandescence and the meteor is seen as a moving streak of light. It is decelerated and usually burns up at a height of 50 km above the ground.

Meteors are often seen disappearing over a nearby hill or other horizon and give

At 15 tons, the Mbozi meteorite, discovered in Tanzania in 1942, is among the largest to have been found. (IOA/Ariadne von Zandbergen)

A bright fireball from the 1999 Leonids meteor shower seen crossing the constellation of Orion. Note the fainter meteor. Tracing the paths back (right) leads to the origin in Leo. (James McGaha)

the impression that they have landed just a few kilometres away, but this is very seldom the case. Usually the meteor is incinerated in the atmosphere. Very occasionally, however, a meteor will survive its passage through the atmosphere and reach the ground, when it is known as a 'meteorite'. The very largest meteorites can leave huge craters such as the vast Vredefort Dome in the Free State, which was formed over two billion years ago. Meteorites are most easily found in desert or semi-desert areas, or may be exposed in the ice in Antarctica. The largest known meteorite is the Hoba meteorite at Grootfontein in Namibia, which weighs 60 tons. Other meteorites may be found in museums.

Meteors can be split into two distinct groups. There are 'sporadic meteors', which occur at random and are thought to have originated from the Asteroid Belt. If you look out on a clear, dark, moonless night at an elevation of about 50° you can

This image, taken in Namibia just before dawn in June 2009, shows the Milky Way and Magellanic Clouds. The zodiacal light is the bright column to the far right, created by sunlight reflecting off interplanetary dust in the plane of the ecliptic. (R. Dobesberger)

expect to see about six such meteors per hour. Millions of years ago, meteors must have been far more abundant, and their bombardment caused the craters on the Moon and some of the planets.

Another distinct group of meteors is associated with comets. These are known as 'shower meteors' and come from the direction of particular constellations at the specific times of the year when the Earth happens to pass across the orbital path of a comet. On these nights many more meteors will be seen, but they will appear to radiate from a single point in the sky. This is a perspective effect, similar to looking down a multi-lane highway or railway line. Meteor showers take their name from the constellation in which they appear, rather than from the comet with which they are associated. For instance, Halley's Comet is associated with the Eta Aquarids in May and the Orionids in October.

Most meteors move through the sky very rapidly, lasting only a fraction of a second, and are popularly called 'shooting stars'. They should not be confused with artificial satellites, which generally move much more slowly, taking a minute or two to cross the sky, and often in a north–south direction. Occasionally, a piece of space junk will re-enter the Earth's atmosphere, creating a spectacular fireworks display, often with red, yellow and green 'sparks'. These can be confused with 'fireballs', a name given to exceptionally bright meteors, brighter than Venus.

OTHER SOLAR SYSTEM PHENOMENA

Zodiacal light

The zodiacal light appears as a cone of light with its base on the horizon and its apex extending perhaps 30° or more along the ecliptic. It can only be seen shortly after darkness in the west and just before dawn in the east, and is most prominent when the ecliptic is perpendicular to the horizon, which is why the best views are obtained from the tropics. From southern Africa, the best viewing times are in the morning sky during March or the evening sky during September. Its brightness varies, but it can often be several times more luminous than the brightest parts of the

Milky Way. To the uninformed observer it can appear as if dawn is breaking, and so the zodiacal light is sometimes called the 'false dawn'.

The zodiacal light is caused by the scattering of sunlight by the interplanetary dust particles concentrated in the plane of the planets. Even here, the dust density is exceedingly low, representing a better vacuum than can be created on the Earth, and the particles are just one micron (0.001 mm) in size.

In 1854 Brorsen discovered a faint patch of light in the midnight sky exactly opposite the Sun. He called it the *gegenschein*, which can be translated as 'counterglow'. Later Brorsen also discovered the zodiacal band that connects the *gegenschein* to the zodiacal light, but both the *gegenschein* and the zodiacal band are very faint and can only be seen on clear, moonless nights from an observing site completely free of light pollution.

Aurorae

Whereas the zodiacal light can only be observed from latitudes below 35°, the aurorae or polar lights can only be seen from high latitudes, close to the geomagnetic poles. In the northern hemisphere they are known as the 'aurorae borealis' and in the south as 'aurorae australis'. They occur in the Earth's atmosphere at a height of about 80 to 160 km and are the result of the ionisation of gases in the atmosphere by charged particles emitted by the Sun. The aurorae typically occur in 'curtains' with green colours for oxygen and red for nitrogen gas. Unfortunately, these events have rarely been glimpsed from the African continent.

An astronaut took this photograph of the Aurora Australis from the space shuttle Discovery in May 1991. To the right of the picture the shuttle's payload bay and tail are visible. (NASA solar system collection)

THE SOLAR SYSTEM 55

THE GALAXY

The Sun is not alone. In fact it has about 2×10^{11} (one hundred thousand million) neighbours in our Galaxy alone. If you go outside on a dark, moonless night you will be able to see several thousand stars in the sky. They are not uniformly distributed, but appear to be concentrated in a band of light we call 'the Milky Way'. With binoculars you can see countless more stars and a host of other objects, some of which will be described later. The Milky Way is not always visible but is best seen in the evening sky in December and June. What we are looking at is a gigantic spiral star city. Unfortunately we get a rather distorted view, as we live within this city. Imagine travelling a few hundred thousand parsecs away from the Earth and looking back. We would see a large flattened disc with an ellipsoidal central bulge, like two fried eggs placed back-to-back. The bright stars in the disc are not uniformly distributed, but are concentrated in several spiral arms.

The Milky Way Galaxy, or 'the Galaxy', is 30 kpc (kiloparsecs, or thousands of parsecs) in diameter and several hundred parsecs thick. The Sun is situated in one of the spiral arms about two-thirds of the way from the nucleus to the edge. When we look out in a direction at right angles to the disc, we see very few stars, because the disc is very thin. However, when we look in the plane of the disc there are many more stars, particularly in the direction of the nucleus, which is located in Sagittarius, a constellation well placed for observation in June. The actual centre of the Galaxy cannot be seen at visible wavelengths, even with the largest telescopes. There is simply too much dust, gas and other absorbing material in the way. Longer wavelengths, namely the infrared and radio, are not so absorbed and reveal the core. By following the orbits of stars in the very centre of the Galaxy, we have been able to confirm the existence of a 'supermassive' nucleus with some four million times the mass of our Sun. Since this nucleus is apparently far smaller than the solar system, yet emits no light, astronomers have concluded it must be a black hole – with such strong gravity that not even light can escape from it. One of the outer spiral arms of the Galaxy is situated in Orion and is well placed for observation in December.

In addition to stars, the spiral arms also contain approximately 10^{10} solar masses in the form of interstellar matter (gas and dust). The arms are areas of active star formation, containing young stars that have been born out of this material. These stars, like the Sun, are hot and luminous and are known as 'Population I' objects. The stars in the nuclear bulge are mainly well advanced in their evolutionary cycle. There is almost no interstellar material or young hot blue stars, and star formation in the nucleus has ceased. These older stars, which are metal poor, are called 'Population II', and are also found in globular clusters spherically distributed in a halo around the Galaxy.

The stars in the galactic disc revolve around the nucleus in approximately circular orbits. The objects nearer the edge take longer to complete one revolution than those close to the nucleus, an effect known as 'differential rotation'. The Sun, which lies about 8 kpc from the centre, takes over 200 million years to make a single orbit. It is currently travelling at 20 km·s^{-1}.

We will now take a close-up look at individual objects within the Galaxy, starting with the stars.

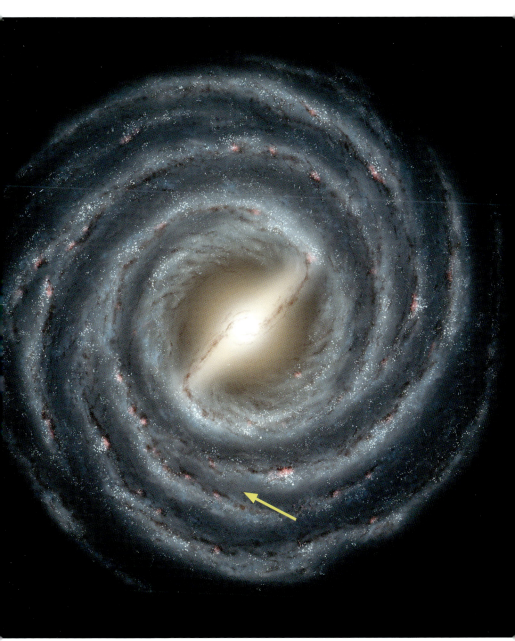

Recent infrared observations with the Spitzer Space Telescope confirm the existence of a central bar of old stars in our Milky Way Galaxy. This artist's impression shows a tightly wound series of spiral arms with our own Sun (see arrow) located some 8 kpc from the centre. The galaxy is an Sbc-type, some 30 kpc in diameter and contains at least 200 billion stars. (NASA/JPL-Caltech/R. Hurt (SSC))

STARS

Stars are other Suns – giant balls of incandescent gas. A casual glance at the brightest stars in the night sky will reveal that they are not all the same colour. In fact, stars vary enormously in size, colour, temperature and physical behaviour. The true understanding of the nature of stars only began with the advent of stellar spectroscopy, just before the turn of the twentieth century. When starlight is passed through a prism and broken down into different colours one can see the usual continuous bright spectrum of red, orange, yellow, green, blue, indigo and violet. Superimposed on this continuum is a series of either dark or bright spectral lines, the 'fingerprints' of an individual star, which are governed primarily by the star's temperature. Stellar spectra are classified into seven main groups, each represented by a letter of the alphabet, that form a temperature sequence. From hottest to coolest, this is O, B, A, F, G, K, M, and can be remembered by the mnemonic Oh Be A Fine Girl (Guy) Kiss Me. Each class is further divided into 10 subclasses designated by a number from 0 to 9, placed after the letter. In addition to temperature classes, stars can also be arranged in luminosity classes, denoted by a Roman numeral (with the first split into two subclasses, a and b). They are:

Ia	Most luminous super-giants
Ib	Less luminous super-giants
II	Bright giants
III	Giants
IV	Sub-giants
V	Main sequence
VI	Sub-dwarfs

Thus the spectral class of a star is described by three terms, a letter and an Arabic numeral to denote its temperature class, and a Roman numeral to denote its luminosity class. The Sun is a G2V star. Examples of some of the brightest stars are given in Appendix 3 (page 100).

A graph comparing the absolute magnitude (the true luminosity) of a star with its spectral class shows that stars fall

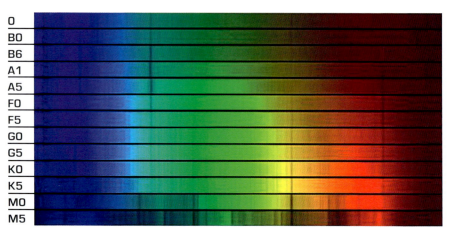

Spectra for the 13 different star classes: the light originating in the inner dense layers of a star is absorbed at specific wavelengths by its cooler outer surface layers. When dispersed by a prism the spectrum shows dark absorption lines, which represent the chemical composition of the star: for instance dark lines in the blue range indicate calcium; in the yellow, sodium. (NOAO/AURA/NSF)

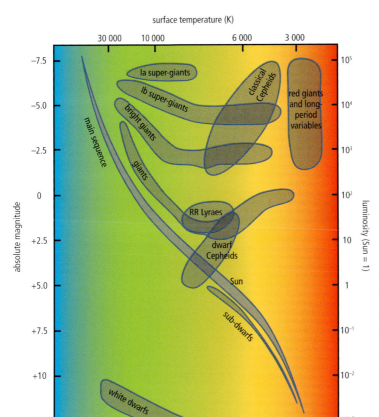

A Hertzsprung-Russell (H-R) diagram plots spectral class or temperature against luminosity or absolute magnitude. Most stars lie on the 'main sequence'.

into distinct groupings. This graph, known as a 'Hertzsprung-Russell (H-R) diagram' after the astronomers who first developed it, shows that about 90% of the stars lie in a narrow band called the 'main sequence', which stretches diagonally across the diagram. The cooler (red) stars lie to the right of the diagram and the hotter (blue) ones to the left. Stars that do not lie on the main sequence also fall into distinct groups such as the super-giants, giants, RR Lyraes and white dwarfs.

Double stars

Our solar system is dominated by a single star, the Sun. However, binary systems, with two stars orbiting each other, are commonplace. There can often be more than two stars, but stable orbits are only possible when pairings take place. For example, our nearest stellar neighbour, the Alpha Centauri System, consists of two bright stars circling each other in about 80 years, with a third, very faint star far out, and apparently circling the other two very slowly. The position of the faint star currently puts it as the member of the trio closest to Earth and hence it has been called 'Proxima Centauri'. The bright 'star' Castor, in the constellation of Gemini, actually consists of no fewer than six suns – arranged in three pairs.

Nearby, widely spaced, binary stars can usually be seen separately in a telescope. For instance, a small telescope easily shows the two bright stars of Alpha Centauri. But it has become obvious that there are many double stars with much smaller spacings, quite impossible to separate visually through a telescope. These can usually be identified as 'spectroscopic binaries': since they lie close together, their orbital velocities are relatively high – enough to cause mild 'redshifting' and 'blueshifting' of spectral features and so to reveal their binary nature.

There are even cases where binary stars lie so close to one another that they distort each other and virtually touch or even interchange material. We usually only know about such configurations when the Earth lies close to their orbital plane, and we view the systems edge-on. More will be said about these binaries in the section that follows.

Variable stars

It has been speculated that very slight decreases in the Sun's energy may have contributed to some of the ice ages on Earth, but on the whole the Sun's output has remained remarkably constant for hundreds of thousands of years. However, some stars behave in a quite different manner, and their brightness changes with time. These variations can be periodic, quasi-periodic or irregular and the variations take place on timescales ranging from a few minutes to many years. The causes can either be extrinsic, meaning that the change in brightness is due to some external factor such as an eclipse, or they can be intrinsic, meaning that the change occurs in the star itself. With modern equipment, measurements of stellar brightness can be made to a precision of 0.001 mag.

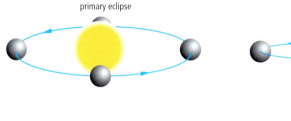

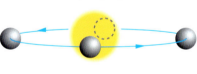

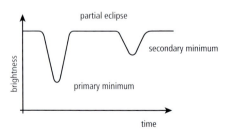

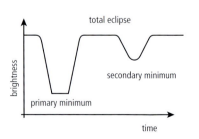

An Algol-type eclipsing variable: a primary eclipse occurs when the smaller star in a well-separated binary pair is hidden by the larger star, and its light can no longer be seen. This produces a significant drop in the total light output. A secondary eclipse occurs when the smaller star passes in front of the larger star. This produces a smaller drop in the total light output.

The most common reason for a star to vary extrinsically is that it is one of a mutually eclipsing binary pair. Algol-type eclipsing variables consist of two well-separated stars whose line of sight from Earth lies close to their orbital plane. Eclipses occur at regular periods: when the brighter star is eclipsed (a 'primary minimum') and when the fainter component is eclipsed (a shallower 'secondary minimum'). Beta Lyrae eclipsing variables are similar, but the stars are so close that tidal and rotational forces distort them into ellipsoids and cause considerable light variations over their surfaces. As the stars rotate on their own axes they show intensity variations, even outside of an eclipse. The similar but even more closely bound Omega Ursae Majoris variables exhibit eclipses with periods as short as 5 hours. This type of star is also called a 'contact binary', because the two stars actually touch.

The most common reason for a star to be an intrinsic variable is because it pulsates. During these pulsations the star expands and contracts, though not necessarily in a simple radial fashion. We shall look at three classes of these stars: 'Cepheids', 'RR Lyraes' and 'Miras'.

Cepheids take their name from their prototype Delta Cephei, an easily observed naked-eye variable that is just below the northern horizon from most of southern Africa. Cepheids are super-giant yellow stars whose brightness varies by about 1 mag over a period that can range from 1 to 100 days.

In 1908 Henrietta Leavitt discovered an important relationship between the period of pulsation of a Cepheid and its luminosity. She noted that the brightest Cepheids in the Small Magellanic Cloud (SMC) have the longest periods. Since all objects in the SMC, a small satellite galaxy to our own, must be at roughly the same distance, those stars with the brightest apparent magnitudes must also have the brightest absolute magnitudes. So, knowing the period, one can find the absolute magnitude, which allows us to calculate the distance to the object.

Fortunately, Cepheids are extremely luminous stars (up to 10^5 brighter than our Sun), and can be seen at great distances. When Cepheids were observed in the Andromeda 'nebula', it was proved beyond doubt that this was an external galaxy. Cepheids occur throughout the nearby galaxies and in globular clusters, and have been extensively observed in order to probe the structure of our Galaxy and nearby systems such as the Magellanic Clouds.

RR Lyrae stars are much more common in globular clusters than Cepheids, and also occur throughout the Galaxy, especially in the central bulge. Their periods range from a third of a day to a day, and brightness varies from 0.5 to 1.5 mag. Their light curve is not symmetrical, but brightens quickly and fades more slowly, an effect that is more pronounced at longer periods. RR Lyraes are useful as they all have the same absolute magnitude of +0.5, regardless of their period. The characteristic light curve allows the stars to be identified and by measuring the average brightness one can determine their distance. The assumption that all RR Lyrae stars have the same absolute magnitude is based on the fact that they all have about the same age, mass and helium content, and have all just started 'burning' helium in their cores.

The Mira variables are classified as long-period variables with periods ranging from several months to almost 2 years, and brightness variations of

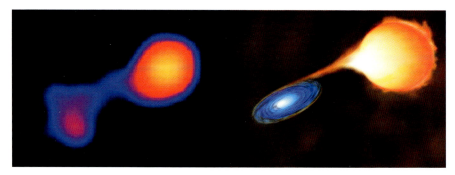

A cool, radially pulsating red giant star, Omicron Ceti or Mira, is 700 times the diameter of the Sun, with an 11-month period. It co-orbits with a rapidly rotating white dwarf that has pulled material off Mira into an accretion disc. The left-hand image is from the Chandra X-ray Observatory and shows an X-ray burst on Mira; the right-hand image is an artist's impression of the system. (NASA/CXO/SAO and impression by M. Weiss)

up to 10 mag. These light variations are so large and take place so slowly that they are ideal targets for visual observations by amateur astronomers. The Mira variables are very cool red giant stars with diameters several hundred times larger than the Sun, but they contain only one solar mass, so the outer layers of the atmosphere must be very rarefied (that is, contain very little gas). The prototype star, Mira or Omicron Ceti, is perhaps the most famous of all the variables, and changes by over 8 mag in 331 days. It reaches mag 1.7 at maximum, when it is a very conspicuous red star.

One of the most useful ways in which amateurs can contribute to modern astronomy is by observing variable stars, especially the irregular variables, which can suddenly brighten or fade without warning. When such events occur professional astronomers can be informed, so that they can study the objects in greater detail.

STELLAR EVOLUTION

Stellar evolution, or the birth, life and death of stars, preoccupied many astronomers during the late nineteenth century. The current theory is that stars form out of interstellar material, gas (chiefly hydrogen) and dust, which come together under their own self-gravitation. As the proto-star collects more and more material its core becomes hotter and hotter as the pressure increases due to the increase in gravity. Stars are in equilibrium: internal core pressure tries to expand while the gravity of the outer layers squeezes the star. Eventually, after about a million years, the core temperature may reach $10^7\,°C$ and nuclear reactions can take place, converting hydrogen into helium. At this point the star enters the main sequence, its position on the H-R diagram being determined by its mass. The more massive the star, the greater its luminosity, the higher up the main sequence it appears, and the more quickly it will evolve. A G2V star like the Sun is expected to have a main-sequence lifetime of about 10^{10} years, while a B0 star may have a main sequence lifetime of just a few tens of millions of years.

The star leaves the main sequence when most of the hydrogen has been converted into helium. At this stage the core starts to contract and becomes much hotter, while the outer layers of the star expand to several hundred times the star's main-sequence diameter. The core stops contracting when it is hot enough for helium to fuse into carbon. There are now two sources of energy generation: nuclear processing of helium into carbon in the core, and of hydrogen into helium in a shell further out. The star has now evolved into a red giant, which is extremely large, very luminous and relatively cool. Further evolution of the star depends on its mass.

A low-mass star like the Sun will evolve into a white dwarf. These stars occupy the lower left part of the H-R diagram (page 59) because they are of very low luminosity and high effective temperature. Nuclear reactions do not take place in white dwarfs, but because their surface areas are so small, they can take hundreds of billions of years to cool. White dwarfs are typically similar in size to Earth and have densities of around 10^9 kg·m^{-3}, or one million times that of water. Stars greater than 1.4 solar masses cannot evolve into white dwarfs unless they lose mass in some way, such as via stellar winds, or if the outer shell can be thrown off to produce a planetary nebula.

Stars greater than 1.4 solar masses will probably die in violent supernova explosions. When very massive stars run out of fuel the outward pressure ceases and the star collapses. This heats up the core igniting a gigantic helium explosion or Type II supernova. Low-mass stars such as white dwarfs in a binary system can accrete matter and thereby exceed 1.4 solar masses. The outward pressure cannot support the excess mass and the carbon core ignites in a Type 1a supernova. These explosions can outshine the entire output of a galaxy for months. The material thrown off forms a nebula; the remaining core contracts into a rapidly rotating neutron star. Type 1a supernovas can be used as 'standard candles' to measure distances, as they have almost identical masses and follow a characteristic light curve, brightening to the same absolute mag -19.3 shortly after the explosion. It is important to observe the peak brightness of the light curve and amateurs play a key role in these observations. Unlike variable stars supernovae can be seen at great distances.

A neutron star is made chiefly of neutrons and is extremely dense: it may be only about 10 km in diameter, yet contain more mass than the Sun. The average density is 10^{16} kg·m^{-3}, which means that a thimbleful of this material would weigh over 10 million tonnes. Pulsars, which were discovered in 1968, are now known to be rapidly rotating neutron stars.

A very massive object may collapse even further and become a black hole. The gravitational forces are so strong that not even light can escape from such an object, and so it cannot be directly observed. A black hole's presence can only be inferred from its gravitational influence on other bodies, or the X-ray radiation emitted as it swallows matter from a companion star.

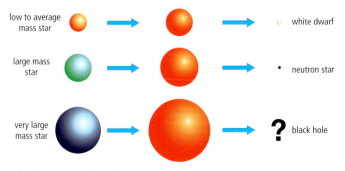

The fate of a star depends on its mass.

INTERSTELLAR MEDIUM

The 'space' between planets, stars and galaxies is not empty. The matter that exists between these objects is called a 'medium'. The 'interplanetary medium' consists of comets, meteors, dust, gas and other debris, while the 'interstellar medium' consists mainly of hydrogen and helium gas and minute dust particles. The density of the Earth's atmosphere at sea level is about 5×10^{19} atoms·cm^{-3}. At the height at which the space shuttle orbits, the density drops to 10^9 atoms·cm^{-3}, considered a 'vacuum' by everyday standards. However, the interstellar medium is a billion times less dense, with just one atom in every cubic centimetre. Such densities are impossible to reproduce in a laboratory, and so the physics of the interstellar medium is of importance to scientists. The Galaxy is so enormous that, even with such low densities, it contains about 10^{10} solar masses of interstellar material, that is, about 10% of its total mass.

Nebulae

The interstellar medium is not uniform. It is concentrated into giant clouds of gas and dust called 'nebulae' (from the Latin word for 'cloud'). The term is used for various objects and was once used of galaxies, since they appeared 'nebulous' in small telescopes, although it is no longer used in this context.

One of the first astronomers to catalogue nebulae was the Frenchman Charles Messier, who published a list of just over 100 objects in 1781. Nebulae were a nuisance to Messier, who was actually interested in comets, which appear similar in a small telescope, and he made the catalogue so as to avoid confusion. However, Messier's catalogue is still in use today, designating each object with the capital letter M before a number in the range 1 to 104: so M1 is the Crab Nebula and M42 is the Orion Nebula. Some of the brighter Messier objects are marked on the accompanying star charts (page 74). Nebulae fall into five main groups: 'emission', 'reflection', 'planetary', 'supernova remnants' and 'dark' nebulae.

'Emission nebulae' are gigantic clouds of gas that have stars embedded within them. These stars are usually very young, hot blue super-giants that have just been born out of the nebulous gas. The gas cloud, which is typically 8 to 20 pc in diameter, absorbs the light from these stars, which mainly emit in the ultraviolet part of the spectrum. This causes the temperature of the gas to rise. The light is re-emitted at a different, but very specific, set of wavelengths that depend on the type of gas present. The spectrum of an emission nebula thus exhibits bright lines from which astronomers can identify the gases present, typically hydrogen, helium, oxygen, sodium, neon and iron. These objects often appear red (hydrogen) or green (oxygen). The most famous emission nebula is the Great Nebula in Orion, which can be seen with the naked eye. Emission nebulae are confined to the spiral arms of the Galaxy, where star birth takes place, and so you will only find them close to the galactic plane. A casual glance with binoculars along the Milky Way near Sagittarius will reveal many such objects.

'Reflection nebulae' contain dust grains that reflect scattered light from nearby stars. They typically appear blue, as blue light is scattered more easily than red light (hence the daytime sky is blue). Because the light is reflected, rather than absorbed, the spectrum of these nebulae is the same as that of the stars that illuminate them. A classic reflection nebula is found in M45, the Pleiades star cluster or Seven Sisters. Although the cluster itself is a fine sight, the nebulosity can only be seen in long-exposure images.

'Planetary nebulae' were given this name because they look like small greenish discs, similar in appearance to Neptune under low magnification. In a high-quality telescope a planetary nebula appears as a ring of gas, principally hydrogen, in the centre of which is a hot star of 50 000 °C or more. The key difference between emission and planetary nebulae is that the former is associated with the birth of a star, while the latter results from the expulsion of the outer shell of an old, dying star.

'Planetary nebulae' are spherical shells of gas, not rings: the central star excites the gas and causes it to shine as the shell expands outwards. By measuring the velocity of expansion of the shell, which is typically 20 km·s^{-1}, and measuring its diameter, typically 0.5 pc, we can deduce the date at which the shell must have been ejected. There are about 1 000 known planetary nebulae and most appear as objects of very small angular size, between an arc second and a few arc minutes. The best-known is M57, the Ring Nebula, in Lyra, which can be seen in the north during the winter. Most planetary nebulae lie close to the galactic plane, with a concentration towards the centre in Sagittarius.

'Supernova remnants' are a by-product of the death of massive stars. A supernova explosion is one of the most violent releases of energy in a galaxy, and may outshine the entire galaxy for months. Supernova explosions are rare in our own Galaxy: five have been recorded in the last millennium. During such an explosion a massive star throws off most of its outer shells of hot gas at extremely high velocities, typically between 10 000 and 20 000 km·s^{-1} The stellar remnant becomes a neutron star and fades, often beyond telescopic detection,

In 1764 Messier discovered the first planetary nebula, the Dumbbell Nebula (M27, NGC 6853), in the constellation Vulpecula at a distance of 0.38 kpc. Its diameter is increasing by 6.8 arc seconds per century, a rate of expansion that suggests it is 3 000 to 4 000 years old. At mag 7.4, it is visible in good binoculars. (Brian Murphy, Butler University/SARA Observatory)

but the gas expands out into space to produce a supernova remnant that is visible for many thousands of years.

There are about 100 known remnants in our own Galaxy, the most famous of which is the Crab Nebula, M1, which is a result of the supernova explosion recorded by Chinese astronomers on 4 July 1054. This nebula is about 2 kpc distant and about 4 pc in diameter, with a mass similar to the Sun's. The star that actually caused the Crab Nebula can still be seen, and radio astronomers discovered in 1967 that it flashes on and off 30 times a second. This type of object is known as a 'pulsar', a rapidly rotating neutron star. The pulsar is slowly spinning down, transferring X-ray energy to the nebula and causing it to shine.

Because supernova explosions are so rare in our own Galaxy, they have been studied mainly in external galaxies. The Large Magellanic Cloud (LMC) has lots of supernova remnants that appear as giant filamentary shells. On 24 February 1987, a supernova explosion was detected in the

LMC, the first in over 300 years, causing a great deal of excitement in the astronomical community. It is called 'SN1987A' as it was the first supernova to be detected anywhere in that year.

'Dark nebulae' are dense (10^3 to 10^4 atoms·cm^{-3}) interstellar clouds, consisting mainly of molecular hydrogen, and appear dark because the starlight from more distant objects cannot pass through them. These nebulae are confined to the plane of the Galaxy. The easiest one to see is the Coal Sack, a prominent dark patch to the side of the Southern Cross. Dark nebulae often occur near bright emission and reflection nebulae. They are thought to be places where stars are forming but that have yet to 'turn on' and illuminate the gas. Dark nebulae occur in a range of sizes. The smallest, 'globules', are about the diameter of the solar system, while the largest are several parsecs in diameter. Other classical examples of dark nebulae are the Horsehead Nebula in Orion (which is one of the most difficult objects to see in a telescope because of the nearby bright star Delta Orionis) and the Cone Nebula in Monoceros.

M57 is a showcase object for the northern hemisphere, located between the two bright stars Beta and Gamma Lyrae. It appears as a faint smudge of light in a small telescope. The central star, a mag 15 white dwarf, requires a much larger telescope. (P. Mack)

STAR CLUSTERS

An inspection of objects along the plane of the Milky Way shows that some stars are grouped into clusters, such as the Pleiades and Hyades in the north and Kappa Crucis in the south. These 'open' or 'galactic' clusters confined to the plane of the Galaxy typically contain between a few hundred and a few thousand well-separated members. The brighter stars are easily seen with the naked eye. Most of the known galactic clusters are within 3 kpc of the Sun, an observational effect because more distant clusters simply merge into the dense starry background. The clusters are often associated with nebulosity, M16 in Sagittarius being a famous example, and the stars are usually of the hot, young O or B spectral type. This suggests that galactic clusters are young and that all of the stars were born at the same time. Despite their similar age, they have a range of mass and luminosity and are important for study.

In binoculars or with the naked eye globular clusters appear as small, fuzzy balls of dim light, but a telescope reveals that they contain hundreds of thousands, even millions, of stars. Seen from Earth, the stars almost appear to be touching each other, but this is just because the clusters are so far away (more than 3 kpc) and not very large (7 to 120 pc). The finest globular cluster in the sky is Omega Centauri (NGC 5139), which is 20 pc in diameter. It is easily visible to the naked eye, as are half a dozen or so other clusters. Other classic examples are 47 Tucana, which appears next to the Small Magellanic Cloud (SMC) but is not associated with it, and M13 in Hercules.

Globular clusters contain only old, well-evolved stars like white dwarfs and red giants, and the presence of these objects and the lack of dust and gas suggest that the globulars may be among the oldest types

The Kappa Crucis Cluster (NGC 4755) is one of the youngest known open clusters with an estimated age of only 7.1 million years. Sir John Herschel described it as a 'casket of variously coloured precious stones'. It is also commonly called the Jewel Box. The brightest star is the M-type super-giant Kappa Crucis. There are about 100 stars in the cluster, which is located just over 2 kpc away. (P. Mack)

At a distance of 2.2 kpc, NGC 6397 is the second closest globular cluster to the Earth. The density of stars in the collapsed core of this cluster is nearly a billion times greater than in our solar neighbourhood. Because the stars are so close to each other they often collide, creating a zoo of exotic objects such as blue stragglers, low mass X-ray binaries, millisecond pulsars, and cataclysmic variables. The cluster contains around 400 000 stars. (Brian Murphy, Butler University, SARA Observatory)

of object known. Unlike galactic clusters, globular clusters are not confined to the plane of the Galaxy but form a spherical halo around it. There are approximately 160 globular clusters in the Galaxy. Larger galaxies, like the Andromeda Galaxy, may have around 500 globulars.

M3 is a bright nearby (10.4 kpc) globular cluster visible in the northern sky. It contains several hundred thousand to a million stars, 10% of them binaries, and its age is estimated to be 11.4 billion years. (Brian Murphy, Butler University/SARA Observatory)

The brightest and largest globular cluster in the Milky Way is Omega Centauri (NGC 5139), which contains around 10 million stars. It is easily visible to the unaided eye. (W. Keel, University of Alabama/SARA Observatory)

NGC 5128 is an irregular galaxy in the M83 group of galaxies. At 4.6 Mpc, it is the nearest 'radio' galaxy. It may have undergone a collision with another member of the group. (W. Keel, University of Alabama/SARA Observatory)

EXTRAGALACTIC ASTRONOMY

When you look out on a clear moonless night, away from the city lights, there appear to be countless thousands of objects visible to the naked eye, but this is only the beginning. In fact, without optical aid, you can see only three objects (the Large and Small Magellanic Clouds and the Andromeda Galaxy) that do not belong to our own Galaxy, the Milky Way. Sit back and reflect on this for a while and try to grasp just how enormous our own Galaxy is.

How far away is the most distant object that the eye can see? Well, it's not just a few hundred million kilometres to the planets, or a few parsecs to the nearest stars, but 687 kpc to a faint smudge of light in the northern constellation of Andromeda. This object is an external galaxy, very much like our own but larger, and is called 'M31', or 'NGC 224', the Andromeda Galaxy. The light that we see now left the Andromeda Galaxy 2 200 000 years ago. It is a sister galaxy to our own Milky Way. Despite its seemingly enormous distance it is one of our nearest neighbours, and we interact with it gravitationally. The Andromeda Galaxy also has a number of companions, the most famous being the elliptical galaxies M32 and NGC 205, as well as a very large number of globular clusters.

Although the existence of external galaxies had long been suspected, it was only during the 1930s that astronomers proved it when Cepheid-type variable stars were observed in the Andromeda Galaxy. The luminosity of these stars varies regularly with time, and by measuring this period one can find the luminosity and hence the distance to the object.

The Large and Small Magellanic Clouds (LMC, SMC) appear as detached portions of the southern Milky Way. They are, however, two small satellite galaxies to our own, located just 46 kpc and 63 kpc away respectively.

We now know of almost 40 galaxies – many very small – that form the Local Group, our own Galaxy being second in size only to the Andromeda Galaxy, which is almost twice as massive. So galaxies

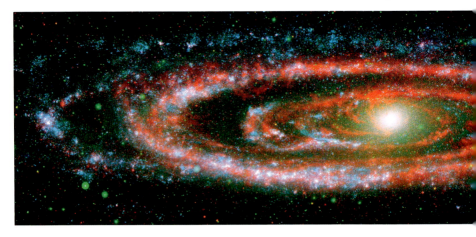

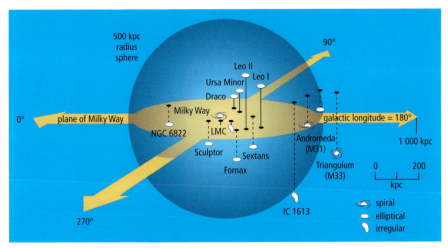

A 3-D representation of the Local Group of galaxies, centred on the Milky Way Galaxy. (Solid lines project above the plane, dotted lines project below the plane.)

have a similar sociology to the stars: they like to form groups or clusters. One important point is that compared to stars, galaxies are very close neighbours relative to their size. The average distance between the stars is millions of stellar diameters, whereas the average distance between the galaxies in the Local Group is just a few dozen galaxy diameters.

The Local Group of galaxies is about 1 Mpc (Megaparsec, one million parsecs) in diameter and it is fairly isolated from more distant galaxies, many of which belong to similar groups. It is an outlying member of the Virgo Supercluster, a collection of thousands of galaxies, whose centre is a dense cluster of galaxies lying in the constellation of Virgo some 16 Mpc away. On a scale this large, the universe exhibits a sponge-like texture, a vast interconnected labyrinth of superclusters percolated by a network of voids. Our own Virgo Supercluster interconnects with a large concentration of galaxies and clusters in Centaurus, including the massive Norma Cluster about 70 Mpc distant. Other superclusters are Coma, centred on the massive Coma Cluster about 100 Mpc away, and Perseus–Pisces, about 70 Mpc out.

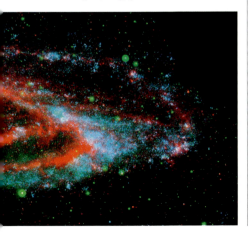

The Andromeda Galaxy is our neighbouring spiral galaxy, yet light from this object takes 2.2 million years to reach us. This is a false-colour composite image comprised of spacecraft data from far-ultraviolet (blue), near-ultraviolet (green) and far-infrared (red) detectors. (NASA/JPL-Caltech)

EXTRAGALACTIC ASTRONOMY

GALAXY CLASSIFICATION

Galaxies can be classified into different groups based on their morphology. The four main divisions are spirals, barred spirals, ellipticals, lenticulars and irregulars.

Our own Milky Way is a spiral galaxy, its true nature disguised by the fact that we live within it. These galaxies have spiral arms that emanate from a nucleus. The spiral arms contain lots of dust and gas and are areas of active star formation. Spirals are classified into three types, Sa, Sb and Sc, to describe the tightness of the winding of the arms. (Sa galaxies have tightly wound arms and Sc types have very loose arms.) A typical spiral galaxy will contain about 10^{11} stars. Galaxies are distributed at random angles. They may appear face-on and show the arms, or they may appear edge-on and show their disc, or at any angle in between.

Barred spirals are similar to normal spirals, except that the arms emanate from either end of a central bar that contains the nucleus. They are classified as SBa, SBb, and SBc in similar fashion to the normal spirals. In 2005 the Spitzer Space Telescope confirmed that our own Galaxy is a barred spiral.

Elliptical galaxies are very symmetrical, and range in shape from spherical (E0) through to highly oblate (E7) systems. Ellipticals do not contain dust and gas. They vary over an enormous range of sizes, from dwarf ellipticals with 10^5 solar masses to super-giant ellipticals. The most famous super-giant elliptical is M87 in the Virgo Supercluster, the largest galaxy known, with a colossal 10^{13} (ten million million) solar masses. Dwarf ellipticals are probably the most abundant galaxies in the universe, while super-giant ellipticals are the rarest.

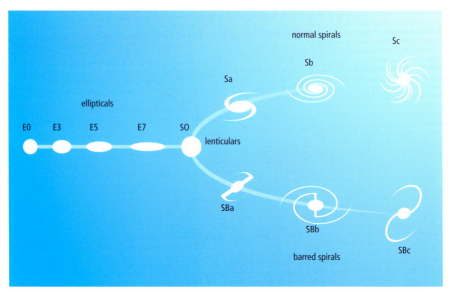

Hubble tuning-fork diagram, showing different morphological types. The sequence was initially believed to show stages of galaxy evolution (moving from left to right). This is now known to be false, but the diagram is still a useful way to classify galaxies. (Irregular galaxies are not shown.)

Lenticular galaxies (shaped like a double-convex lens) show evidence of a disc, but no spiral structure. They are very similar to ellipticals, and like them are found mainly in dense clusters.

Irregular galaxies, as their name suggests, have no systematic structure, but they are usually much less massive than our own Galaxy. One of the most famous irregular galaxies is the Large Magellanic Cloud.

With modern detectors, principally sensitive charge-coupled device (CCD) cameras, astronomers have now detected many thousands of millions of galaxies. They represent the basic building blocks of the universe.

NGC 1566 is a spiral galaxy in the constellation Dorado. Mature stars emit blue light, while the spiral arms are red. There is a great deal of dust here as this is the site of active star formation. The nucleus is blue and luminous, which indicates that this is a Seyfert galaxy, which emits intense radiation from an active nucleus. (NASA/JPL-Caltech)

A small percentage of galaxies possess 'active nuclei', apparently arising from the presence of super-massive black holes about a billion times more massive than our Sun. Many giant ellipticals, which look quite benign in optical telescopes, are seen by radio telescopes to eject enormous jets of matter into pairs of lobes on either side of the galaxy. By contrast, active spiral galaxies show highly luminous nuclei, which on occasion can outshine the rest of the galaxy. The nature of the light from these nuclei shows that it is 'non-thermal', that is to say it has not been produced by stars of any sort. Spirals with active nuclei of modest luminosity are known as 'Seyfert galaxies', after the astronomer who first called attention to them. The more extreme examples are known as 'quasars'. Quasars are exceedingly luminous galaxies that can be seen at very great cosmological distances, placing them among the most remote objects known.

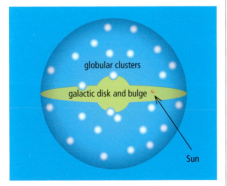

Globular clusters form a spherical halo around the galaxy, 30 kpc in diameter.

EXTRAGALACTIC ASTRONOMY   71

THE EXPANDING UNIVERSE

The universe is known to be expanding. Groups of galaxies are separating from each other as the space between them expands, like a rubber sheet stretching. This has been taking place continuously since the origin of the universe, 13.7 billion years ago. The universe began in a very hot, very dense state and the subsequent expansion is usually dubbed the 'big bang'. The expansion has allowed the universe to cool, so that superclusters, galaxies, stars and planets have been able to form. According to Hubble's law, the further away a galaxy is, the faster it appears to be moving away from us. We

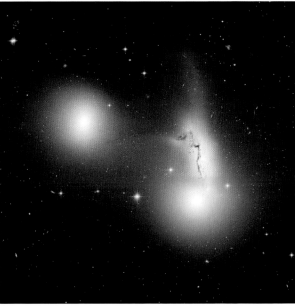

The Hickson Compact Group 90 comprises a small spiral galaxy caught between two elliptical galaxies. The elliptical galaxies will ultimately swallow up the smaller galaxy. (NASA)

are not in a privileged position – the same phenomenon would be experienced no matter which galaxy we inhabited. The velocity of recession is directly proportional to the distance to the object, and the constant relating the two is known as 'Hubble's constant', H. Hubble's law is often expressed as $v = H_0 d$, where v is the velocity of the object in km·s^{-1} and d is the distance in megaparsecs (Mpc). The best estimate of Hubble's constant is currently 70.8 km·s^{-1} Mpc^{-1}. To put this another

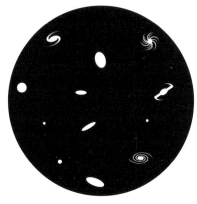

The universe is known to be expanding. The distance between the galaxies is increasing with time, but the size of the individual galaxies remains constant.

way, for every million parsecs of distance between us and an object, its recessional velocity is greater by 70.8 km·s^{-1}.

The recession of the galaxies implies that there is a limit to the distance to which we can observe, because beyond this limit the galaxies would be moving away at the speed of light. The most distant object ever observed (as of 2009) was a gamma-ray burst from a stellar explosion about 13.1 billion light years away, which occurred just 630 million years after the big bang.

Observations of the rotation of spiral galaxies show that most stars orbit at roughly the same speed (rather than moving more slowly at larger radial distances), implying that they are dominated by 'dark matter' that neither emits nor scatters light or other electromagnetic radiation. Without this matter the galaxies would simply fly apart.

A gravitational lens occurs when light from a very distant source is bent around a very massive intervening object. Such observation also imply the existence of dark matter.

Using Type 1a supernova as standard candles and measuring their redshifts, two groups of astronomers have independently shown that the expansion of the universe is accelerating and were awarded the 2011 Nobel prize in physics. This acceleration is being driven by a force called 'dark energy'. The amount of energy required to fit the observed acceleration can be calculated.

We now know that roughly 70% of the universe is made of dark energy, 25% is dark matter and only 5% is the 'normal' matter we see.

Further observations as well as particle physics experiments on Earth are required to understand the exact nature of dark matter and dark energy.

Possible scenarios for the expansion (and contraction) of the universe:
● *The orange curve represents a closed high-density universe that expands for several billion years then collapses under its own weight.*
● *The green curve represents a flat critical-density universe in which the expansion rate slows down and the curve becomes ever more horizontal.*
● *The blue curve shows an open low-density universe whose expansion is also slowing down but not as much.*
● *The red curve shows a universe that is accelerating, driven by dark energy. Modern observations suggest that this is the correct model.*

Note that the curves of all of these universe scenarios meet at time = 'now'.

STAR CHARTS

Finding your way around the night sky can be a difficult and confusing task. One problem is that the stars rise (and set) approximately 4 minutes earlier each day, as a result of the Earth orbiting the Sun. The traditional approach is to provide a series of charts that show the entire sky, usually in two hemispheres, for different times of the year. However, interesting objects are not evenly distributed across the sky, so a different approach is used here: star charts showing the most popular areas of the sky are presented together, with a matching photograph in each case. This makes it much easier to identify constellations, because you have a 'real' view of the sky. The charts are designed for 30° S but can be used at any location between 20° S and 40° S. Note that each image is 180 degrees – far more than the eye can take in: imagine stretching your hands out left–right as far as you can. Keeping your shoulders still, look to the fingers at your left, then to your right. This is the extent of the camera view.

First let's take a look at the chart below, which shows the entire path of the ecliptic. (See Appendix 2, p. 99, for the table of abbreviations.) This chart is different from all the others because it shows the entire sky around the equator, including that which is beneath your feet. The red line is the ecliptic and the point at which this line crosses from south to north is, by definition, zero hours. We have split the map not at 0h but rather at 12h because splitting it at 0h breaks up the constellation of Pegasus. The

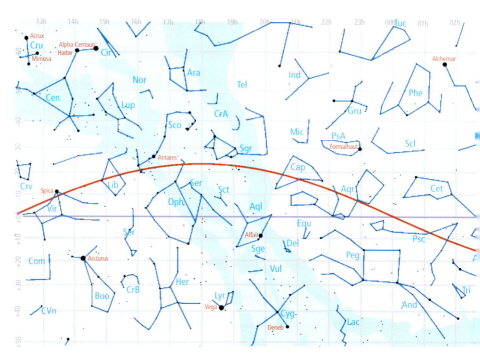

chart is divided into 24 hours when each hour is also 15°. These are lines of right ascension. The declination lines are plotted every 10° with south at the top because the chart is designed for use in the southern hemisphere. The plane of the Milky Way is indicated by the distinct blue band. The part of the band that passes through Orion (at 6h) is overhead at midnight in summer and the part that passes through the Scorpius–Sagittarius region (at 18h) is overhead at midnight in winter. Face north while using the ecliptic chart as the ecliptic is always to the north of your location.

During the course of a whole night a constellation that is rising in the east will transit at midnight and set in the west in the early morning. This should come as no surprise – it's what the Sun does each day. What may not be so obvious is that a rotation occurs during the night. Suppose that Orion is rising in the east. Hold the chart on its side so that 13h is at the top and 12h is at the bottom and face east. This will be the approximate orientation of Orion. Rigel is to your right and Betelgeuse to your left. Now slowly rotate the book as you turn to the north, until it becomes horizontal. Continue to rotate the book while turning west. Now 12h is at the top of the chart. So the important lesson here is that the orientation of the constellations changes as they move across the sky. The easiest way to learn the sky is to recognise a few prominent constellations and then use those as stepping stones to identify fainter, more obscure patterns.

The images presented with the charts were obtained with a very simple set-up. A Canon 5D camera with a 15 mm lens was mounted on a tripod. Most exposures are 30 seconds' duration. The star charts have been designed to cover the same field.

The Messier Catalogue objects are also depicted, together with a few very bright southern objects. These are the most spectacular of the open clusters, globular clusters, planetary nebula, diffuse nebula and galaxies. Many of them can be seen in binoculars or a small telescope.

The best time to observe is when the Moon is absent, and from a site where there is minimal light pollution. In really brightly lit areas the Milky Way may not be visible at all.

The time quoted as 'midnight' in the maps does not mean 00h00 local time. It means 'the middle of the night', halfway between sunset and sunrise. This may be up to 90 minutes away from local time, depending on your longitude compared with the longitude of your time zone, and any daylight savings.

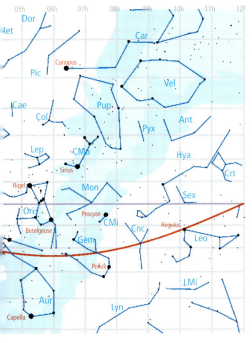

This chart shows the entire path of the ecliptic.

Chart 1 Facing north: October sunrise, January midnight, March sunset

Orion (Ori), which is the best-known constellation and is visible from anywhere on Earth, dominates the northern view. The Milky Way runs almost vertically through the scene and many fine objects can be viewed with binoculars. Showcase examples are the Pleiades Cluster (M45), the Orion Nebula (M42) and the Hyades Custer just to the left of Aldebaran in Taurus (Tau).

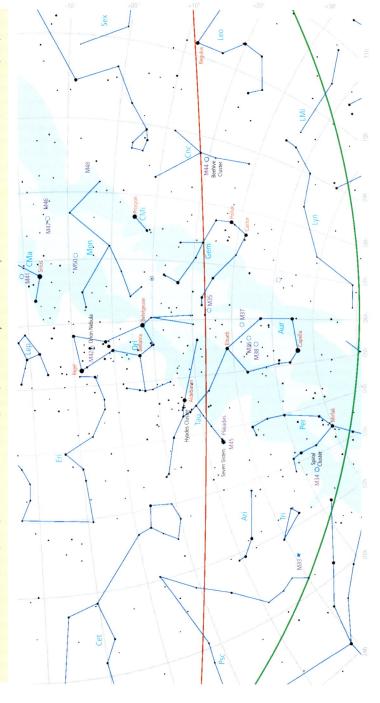

76 STAR CHARTS

Chart 2 Facing north: January sunrise, March midnight, June sunset

The bright stars on the horizon are part of Ursa Major (UMa). The brilliant red star Arcturus can be used to find Boötes and the rather distinctive northern crown (Corona Borealis (CrB)). The constellation of Leo is one of the easiest to find. Because Regulus and Spica both lie very close to the ecliptic the patterns are often confused by the presence of bright planets. Mars and Saturn were in the area when this image was taken; other planets may be visible on the night when you are observing.

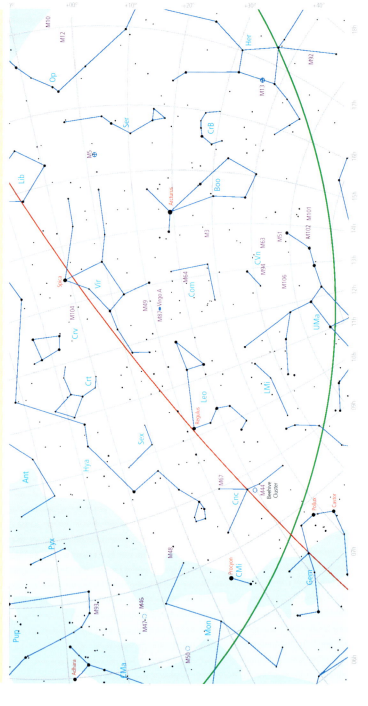

78 STAR CHARTS

Chart 3 Facing north: June sunrise, October midnight, December sunset

The bright stars Vega, Deneb and Altair form the 'summer triangle' as these stars are overhead during summer in the northern hemisphere. The 'square of Pegasus' (Peg) can be used to find the Andromeda Galaxy (And, M31), which is just visible to the unaided eye from a dark site. Numerous globular clusters and open clusters are easily visible with binoculars. Try searching from Andromeda through Cygnus (Cyg) and along the Milky Way to the Serpens (Ser)–Scutum (Sct) region.

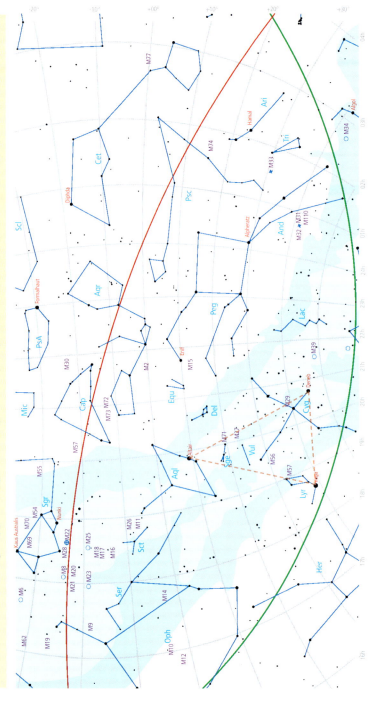

80 STAR CHARTS

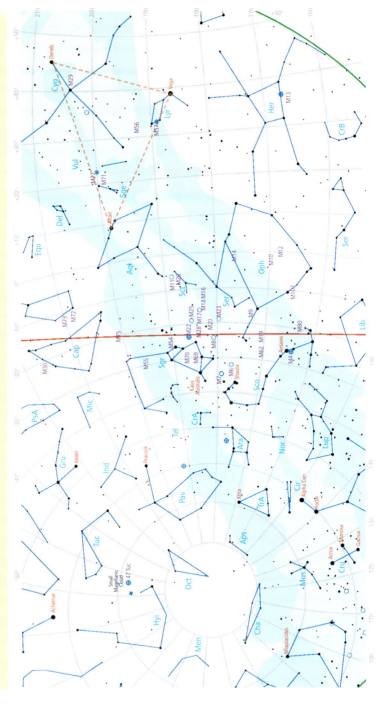

Chart 4 Facing west: April sunrise, July midnight, October sunset

The summer triangle of Altair–Deneb–Vega is setting in the northwest. The galactic centre dominates the western sky. The ecliptic is almost perpendicular to the horizon, and this is a good time to look for the zodiacal light if you are at a dark observing site.

82   STAR CHARTS

Chart 5 Facing west: October sunrise, January midnight, April sunset

Orion (Ori) is lying on its side and the Pleiades Cluster (M45) has almost set. The Milky Way stretches across the view to the Southern Cross (Cru) high in the south and is highlighted by numerous very bright stars.

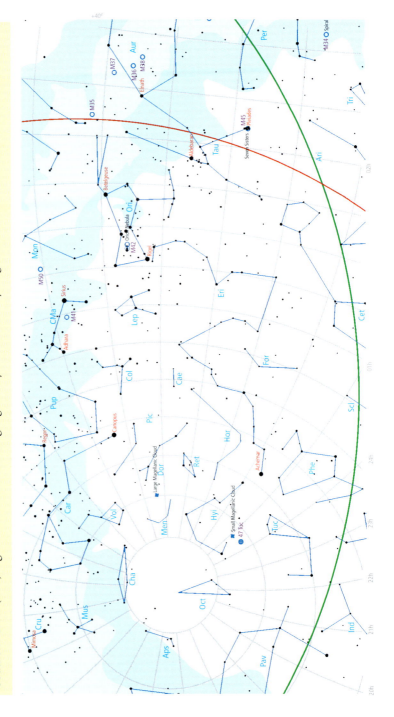

84   STAR CHARTS

STAR CHARTS

Chart 6 Overhead, feet facing east: June sunrise, October midnight, December sunset

The Andromeda Galaxy (And) on the northern horizon is the most distant object visible to the unaided eye. Overhead there are very few bright stars as you're looking out of the plane of the Milky Way. Be sure to find the globular cluster 47 Tuc.

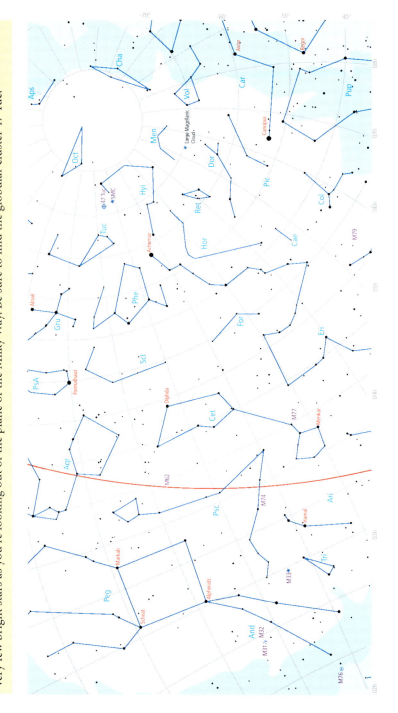

86 STAR CHARTS

Chart 7 Facing south: January sunrise, March midnight, June sunset

The Southern Cross (Cru) is at its highest point in the sky, while the Galactic Centre is rising in the far southeast. The Small Magellanic Cloud is at its lowest point and the Large Magellanic Cloud is setting.

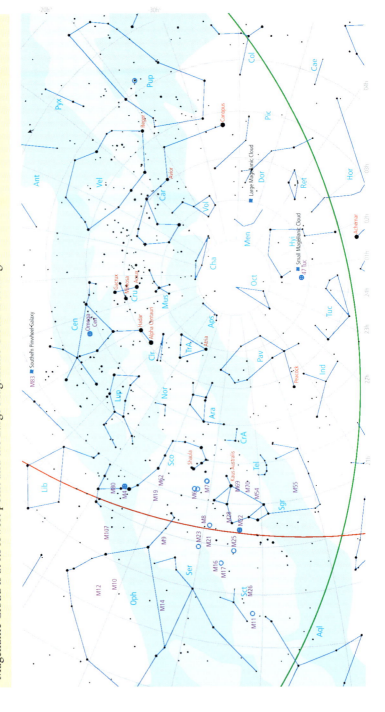

88 STAR CHARTS

Chart 8 Facing south: August sunrise, December midnight, February sunset

The Southern Cross (Cru) has just passed lower culmination and the Magellanic Clouds are high above the celestial pole. The accompanying image shows the False Cross in red and the Southern Cross in green. Note that only the Southern Cross points to the south celestial pole (yellow +). The pointer stars Hadar and Rigel Kent (Alpha Cen) are close to the horizon. For observing sites north of about -30° the constellation is not circumpolar.

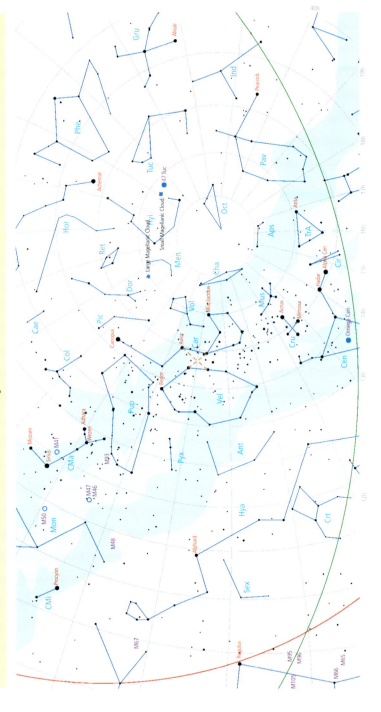

90 STAR CHARTS

SELECTED INTERESTING OBJECTS

The numbers in brackets after a constellation name, for example **Andromeda** (3, 6), are references to chart numbers. So, if you face north at around midnight in October – as per Charts 3 and 6 – you will see Andromeda at the point at which it is highest in the sky and most visible. The object may also be shown on other charts, but it may not be as well placed for observation. (Note NGC = New General Catalogue, the best known catalogue of nebulae, star clusters and galaxies; M = Messier Catalogue, the celestial bodies charted by Charles Messier. Other abbreviations and units of measurement used in this list are explained in Appendix 1.)

Andromeda (3, 6). Although it is poorly placed for observation from southern Africa, most amateur astronomers turn their instruments towards one object in this constellation, the Andromeda Galaxy, M31 (NGC 224). This faint smudge of light 2.2 million light years away (780 kpc) is just visible to the unaided eye. Binoculars show a spiral galaxy. Look for its nearby companion, M32.

Aquarius (3, 6). This constellation contains the planetary nebula NGC 7009, known as the Saturn Nebula because of its resemblance to that planet, which is situated 1° W of Nu Aquarii (ν Aqr). To see it you will need a 250 mm telescope. First observed by Herschel in 1782, it is mag 8, 8.25" dia., small but very bright. The central star is mag 12. Two interesting globular clusters, M2 and M72, are located in Aquarius. M2 is partially resolved into individual stars in a 200 mm telescope. It contains nearly 200 RR Lyrae and several Cepheid variables.

M72 is considerably fainter and can just be resolved with a 250 mm telescope. The best southern hemisphere meteor shower, the η (Eta) Aquariids, occurs in early May, when over 30 meteors can be seen per hour, if the Moon is absent.

Aquila (3, 4). Eta Aquilae (η Aql) is the third brightest Cepheid in the sky after Polaris and Delta Cephei (δ Cep), both of which are invisible from southern Africa. It has a period of 7.18 days and varies between mag 4.5 and 3.7.

Ara (4, 7). The bright open cluster NGC 6193 is embedded in a bright and dark nebula, NGC 6188. This object is in a rich area of the Milky Way and is easy to find with binoculars.

Auriga (1). Capella is the sixth brightest star in the sky and the most northerly first-magnitude star visible from these latitudes. Three interesting open clusters, M36, M37 and M38, are found in the constellation.

Bootes (2). The red giant star Arcturus is a useful 'landmark'. It is the fourth brightest star and can easily be identified by its colour.

Cancer (1). M44, the Beehive or Praesepe open cluster, lies on the ecliptic and is frequently occulted by the Moon. It is one of the largest and nearest clusters and, at mag 4.5, can easily be seen without optical aid. Binoculars show it very well, as it is over 1° dia. M67 is another open cluster in Cancer, but is much less spectacular, at mag 7 and 15' dia. It lies 1.8° W of Alpha Cancri (α Cnc).

Canes Venatici (2). A small and rather obscure constellation lying west of Bootes, it contains a large number of galaxies belonging to the Virgo cluster. The main object of interest is a mag 6, 18' dia. globular cluster, M3. lt comprises mainly mag 11 stars and is a fine object to view using at least a 150 mm telescope. M3 contains around 200 variable stars, more than any other cluster, and it is exceedingly rich in very faint stars.

Canis Major (1, 5, 8). Sirius, the Dog Star, is the brightest star in the night sky, and one of the closest at 2.64 pc. It may possibly have been red in the past, but is now a definite blue-white of spectral class A1, some 23 times more luminous than the Sun. Sirius is a double star, and its companion, Sirius B or the Pup, is a white dwarf that orbits its parent once every 50 years. The separation varies between 3" and 11.5", the last minimum occurring in 2000. It is an exceedingly difficult object to spot, mainly because of the brilliance of Sirius, but it can be detected in a 250 mm telescope. Members of the Dogon tribe of Mali, Africa, worship Sirius and claim to have been familiar with Sirius B and to have known of its 50-year period for a long time. It seems likely, however, that they were told of its existence by a French scientist in the 1930s. Just 4° S of Sirius is the open cluster M41, mag 6, 30' dia., which is easily visible to the naked eye. This area of the Milky Way is very rewarding for an observer with binoculars.

Canis Minor (1, 8). The brightest star in this constellation is Procyon, which is another double star with a white dwarf companion. Unlike Sirius B, which is visible in a 250 mm telescope, a very large telescope is required to glimpse Procyon's secondary, which is 15 000 times fainter than Procyon and separated by just 1.25". It is the second closest white dwarf system to the Sun.

Capricornus (3, 6). This constellation lies on the ecliptic. The main object of interest is the globular cluster M30, at mag 8, 6' dia. Most stars in this globular cluster are around mag 12.

Carina (7, 8). This constellation is almost circumpolar. A treasure chest of interesting objects lies in this rich part of the Milky Way, including Canopus (α Car), the second brightest night-time star visible from Earth. The old constellation of the Ship was broken up into smaller sections of which Carina is the keel. The other parts are 'Vela' (sail), 'Puppis' (stern) and 'Pyxis' (compass box). Two of the stars form part of the 'False Cross'. The main object of interest to the casual observer is Eta Carinae (η Car), a nova-like variable embedded in a very bright rich nebula, NGC 3372. This nebula is crossed by dark lanes, splitting the bright sections into little islands. One of the dark lanes looks like a keyhole and it is thus often called the Keyhole Nebula. It is 80' dia., and the entire complex is illuminated by η Car, the most likely candidate for a supernova explosion in our own Galaxy – considered by the author to be the finest spectacle in the entire sky. Just 3° WNW lies NGC 3532, one of the best examples of an open star cluster (discovered in 1752 from South Africa), but the entire region can be studied for countless hours with a small telescope.

Centaurus (7). A very famous southern constellation. The brightest star, Rigel Kentaurus, is often called Alpha Centauri or simply α Cen. In a small telescope it appears as a beautiful binary. However, it is actually a triple star system, the third member of which, Proxima Cen, is famous for being the nearest star to our own Sun. The distance was first measured by Henderson at the Cape of Good Hope in 1839, just two months after

Bessel measured the first stellar parallax in the northern hemisphere. Modern estimates put its distance at 1.3 pc. It is one of 'The Pointers' that point towards the Southern Cross, the other being Hadar (which is also known as Beta Centauri or, simply, β Cen). Centaurus contains two other splendid objects for professional and amateur study. The first is Omega Centauri, or ω Cen (NGC 5139), the finest example of a globular cluster in the entire sky. It is very easy to see with the naked eye and was catalogued by Ptolemy nearly 1 800 years ago. It contains over 1 000 000 stars and appears 30' dia. visually, but is much larger on deep-exposure photographs. In the core of the cluster the star density is about 25 000 times greater than that near the Sun, with an average separation of only 0.3 pc. It contains more variable stars than any other globular except for M3, and it is the second nearest globular to Earth at a distance of about 5 kpc (the nearest being NGC 6397 in Ara, which is much fainter and is not marked on the charts). Only 4.5° N lies the famous radio galaxy Centaurus A (Cen A), a bright irregular galaxy (see page 71) 10' dia., mag 7.2, which is seen 'edge-on' with a central dust lane. Although it is visible in binoculars, a 250 mm telescope is required to show finer detail.

Cetus (1, 3, 6). This constellation contains Mira, the 'wonderful star', a long-period variable. Mira ranges between mag 3 and mag 9.5 with a period of 331 days. In 1779 it rose to mag 1, almost as bright as Aldebaran. Mira can be observed with binoculars throughout its cycle. Also in Cetus are M77, which is a spiral galaxy of mag 10 and the brightest in a group of three galaxies; and NGC 908, another spiral galaxy and one that has thick arms. With modest equipment over 50 galaxies are visible in Cetus.

Corvus (2). A distinctive, easily recognisable pattern. Corvus contains the Ringtail Galaxy, NGC 4038, which formed when two galaxies collided.

Crux (7). A tiny constellation that is well known because it points to the south celestial pole. Visible for most of the year, the bottom star in the cross, Acrux, is a beautiful double of mag 1.58 and 2.09, separation 4,5". Herschel's 'Jewel Box', NGC 4755 or Kappa Crucis (κ Cru) is a glorious multi-coloured cluster. The 'Coal Sack' lies next to the bright star Acrux and is a dark nebula, obscuring the starlight from the more distant Milky Way.

Dorado (7). Contains the Large Magellanic Cloud (LMC), the nearest external galaxy. The brightest nebula in the LMC is 30 Doradus (30 Dor), or the 'Tarantula Nebula', which lies away from the main part of the LMC. The supernova 1987A erupted just to the side of 30 Dor. The LMC contains numerous clusters and nebula and is a favourite subject for astrophotographers. The galaxy NGC 1566 is a classic spiral and is a good object to observe with a larger telescope.

Fornax (1, 5). Contains a cluster of 18 galaxies. NGC 1097 is a barred spiral.

Gemini (1). Easily found by locating the 'heavenly twins', Castor and Pollux, just 4.5° apart. Castor is the finest double star in the north, mag 2.0 and 2.8, separation 2". M35 lies at the Orion end of Gemini and is a fine open cluster containing about 120 stars in a 30' dia.

Grus (8). This distinctive constellation is well out of the Milky Way and contains over 30 galaxies that are detectable with amateur equipment, including the barred spirals NGC 7552 and NGC 7582, both mag 11.7.

Hercules (3, 4). Contains the best globular cluster in the northern sky, M13, which is just visible with the naked eye. In binoculars it is 10' dia. M92, a much fainter globular, is also visible in this constellation.

Hydra (2). A large and difficult constellation. Contains many galaxies including M83. At mag 8 it is one of the brightest in the south, a superb multi-armed spiral. This galaxy has a very high supernova rate. M68 is a fine globular in telescopes of 150 mm aperture or larger.

Leo (2). This is one of the few constellations that looks anything like the creature depicted, although the lion is upside-down as seen from southern Africa! Regulus or Alpha Leonis (α Leo), the brightest star in the constellation, has a companion, mag 7.9, separation 177", which can be seen with binoculars mounted on a tripod. A large telescope will show that the companion is itself a double, the other component being mag 13. Leo contains over 70 galaxies that are visible with modest equipment. There are no clusters or nebulae, the constellation being close to the north galactic pole. Interesting galaxies in Leo include the M65/M66 pair of spirals, which are 21' apart. M95/M96 is another pair of bright spirals, about 9° E of Regulus. M95 is barred.

Libra (2). NGC 5897 is a very loose-structured globular cluster of mag 10, 8.5' dia., and is easily resolvable in a small telescope.

Lyra (3, 4). A far northern constellation, easily found by locating Vega, the fifth brightest star in the sky. M57, the Ring Nebula, is the classical planetary nebula. The low altitude requires a 250 mm or larger telescope. M56 is a mag 8. 5, 5' dia. globular cluster.

Monoceros (1). This constellation is rich in nebulae and open clusters, being in the plane of the Galaxy. R Monocerotis (R Mon) is a peculiar star in Monoceros because it is enveloped in a nebula, called 'Hubble's Variable Nebula'. It varies in size and brightness, but is around mag 10. NGC 2244 is a cluster that is embedded in the Rosette Nebula, which is a fine object for viewing with a small telescope or binoculars as it is visible to the naked eye, 80' dia. NGC 2264 is a large scattered cluster, to the south of which lies a dark conical feature, the Cone Nebula.

Ophiuchus (3, 4). A large, rich constellation that divides Serpens into two areas. M9, M10, M12 and M14 are all fine globular clusters within Ophiuchus. The Milky Way is magnificent in this region.

Orion (1, 5). Perhaps the most famous constellation, being visible from both hemispheres and easily recognisable. M42, the 'Great Nebula in Orion', is the finest example of a nebula in the sky, only rivalled by Eta Carinae (η Car). A small telescope used in a dark moonless sky will reveal most of its features. In the heart of the nebula are four closely spaced stars forming the 'trapezium', but larger telescopes will reveal the asterism as six stars. M78 is 2.3° NE of the eastern star in Orion's 'belt'. It is a bright part of the general nebulosity that pervades Orion.

Pavo (6). NGC 6752, which lies within Pavo, is one of the finest globular clusters in the sky – and the seventh brightest. It is third largest in angular size, being 42' dia. on long exposure photographs. Binoculars will show it as a 15' dia., mag 7 object.

Pegasus (3, 6). The body of the flying horse forms the 'Great Square', a prominent feature in the northern spring skies. Pegasus looks like a horse, but unlike Leo it actually appears the right way up as seen from southern Africa. It contains a fine globular cluster, M15, which has a very condensed core. The object is in the same binocular field as the bright star Enif, the nose of the horse. Also look for the tiny but very distinctive constellation Delphinus, just to the west of this field.

Perseus (1). The only object worthy of note from these latitudes is Algol, or Beta Persei. Algol is the most famous eclipsing binary.

Pisces (3, 6). This constellation is easily found by 'star hopping' from Pegasus. M74 is a very fine face-on spiral of the Sc type, located 1.5° E of Epsilon Piscium (ϵ Psc). It is, however, one of the faintest Messier objects at mag 11.0 and 9' dia.

Sagittarius (4, 7). The centre of our own Galaxy lies in Sagittarius and it is a treasure chest of cosmic wonders. Even the naked-eye observer cannot fail to be amazed at the wealth and beauty of objects in this spectacular area of the Milky Way, which is the envy of northern hemisphere observers. Some of the best objects to observe are the globular clusters M22, M28, M54, M55, M69, M70 and NGC 6553, of which M22 is the finest. M22 can be found just to the west of the Milk Dipper. The area is rich in gaseous nebula including M8, M17 and M20. M8 is the Lagoon Nebula, a mag 5 object measuring 80' × 40', surrounding the open cluster NGC 6350, which contains many mag 7 stars. M17 is the Swan Nebula or Omega Nebula, which is slightly fainter and half the size of M8, but still very prominent. Just over the border in Serpens lies M16. The Trifid Nebula, M20, is the best in the area. Three dark dust lanes split the Trifid Nebula into four distinct bright segments, the total size being about 25' dia.

Scorpius (4). Straddling the ecliptic and the galactic equator, Scorpius is one of the most famous southern constellations. Antares (α Sco) is the 15th brightest star and is very red, rivalled only by Betelgeuse in Orion. Antares means 'the rival of Mars', and, because it lies close to the ecliptic, it is often confused with Mars. The 2016 opposition will be very close. Just 1.3° W lies the obvious naked-eye globular star cluster M4. Just to the north of M4 is M80, and it can be seen in the same 7 × binocular field. At the Sagittarius end of the constellation lie two open star clusters, M6 and M7, both easy naked-eye objects containing about 50 stars. Note that both Sagittarius and Scorpius contain very few galaxies, because they are obscured by the Milky Way.

Sculptor (6, 8). This constellation contains many fine galaxies including NGC 55, a superb, bright, edge-on spiral nearly 30' dia. A 250 mm reflector in dark skies starts to reveal its true splendour. It is one of the closest galaxies outside the Local Group. Another large galaxy is NGC 253, the brightest member of the 'Sculptor Group', which includes NGC 300 and NGC 7793. This may be the nearest group of galaxies outside the Local Group. NGC 288 is a globular cluster, the only object of interest in Sculptor that is not a galaxy.

Serpens (3). Although it is recognised as just one constellation, Serpens is split into two parts by Ophiuchus. In its western part, 'Serpens Caput', lies M5, one of the finest globular clusters visible in binoculars. In its eastern part, 'Serpens Cauda', lies M16, a truly spectacular nebula illuminated by a brilliant young cluster.

Taurus (1). Aldebaran, the eye of the bull, is a red giant star. Nearby are two famous open star clusters: the Hyades and the Pleiades. The latter is also known as M45 or the 'Seven Sisters' and is the easiest naked-eye cluster to be found in the sky. Telescopes do not show it very well, because it is simply too big. See how many stars you can count with the unaided eye and then explore the field with binoculars. Finding the Pleiades was used as a measure of eyesight in antiquity. Some observers mapped out over a dozen stars before the invention of the telescope, but most people see six or seven. If you can only make out five stars, then see an optician! The Crab Nebula, M1, is located in Taurus. The author remembers purchasing his first telescope, which had on the side of its box a picture of the Crab with all its fine filaments. It barely showed this feeble object, the first Messier object he observed, which was a big disappointment. Try a telescope that is 250 mm or larger for a reasonable view, but note that the filaments can only be seen with very large telescopes or sensitive cameras.

Triangulum (1, 3). Contains one of the nearest spirals, M33, 'the Pinwheel'. This is a showcase object for northern observers, and is worth trying to find from the southern hemisphere, despite its low altitude.

Triangulum Australe (1). A small but distinctive constellation containing the planetary nebula NGC 5979. It is almost stellar in appearance, 8" dia. and mag 13. A large telescope is required to view this nebula.

Tucana (6, 8). Tucana is the home of the Small Magellanic Cloud (SMC), a galaxy in the Local Group that is easy to spot with the naked eye. The SMC also contains a number of prominent clusters visible in modest telescopes. Some 2.5° W of the SMC lies the spectacular globular cluster NGC 104, or 47 Tuc. It is rivalled only by Omega Centauri (ω Cen) and is very obvious to the naked eye. Most of the stars here are fainter than mag 11 and a modest telescope is required to resolve them into individual points of light. The cluster is unusual in that it contains almost no RR Lyrae variables and it also contains a pulsar and hundreds of X-ray sources. It may well be a young example of a globular cluster.

Vela (8). Together with stars in Carina, Vela forms the 'False Cross'. It contains a bright (mag 8.2) planetary nebula, NGC 3132, measuring 84" × 52" and has a mag 10 central star. The area is rich in open clusters including the mag 5.5 object NGC 2547.

Virgo (2). The constellation contains over 200 galaxies visible with modest equipment, including members of the Virgo Supercluster. M84 and M87 are two of the largest members of the supercluster. M87 is an ellipsoidal that probably contains a massive black hole and is a strong radio source. A small telescope will show M87 as a mag 10, 3' dia. E1-type elliptical galaxy. M61 is a fine face-on spiral, while M104 is a famous edge-on spiral, the Sombrero. M104 was the first galaxy to have its redshift measured. It is a fine sight in a modest telescope, showing a distinct central dust lane.

Vulpecula (3, 4). This constellation contains M27, the brightest planetary nebula in the entire sky. Also called the 'Dumbbell Nebula' because it looks like two hazy balls in contact, it measures 2' x 5' and is mag 8 with a mag 13.5 central star. It is one of the nearest planetary nebulae to the Sun.

APPENDIX 1: Mathematical expressions, constants and the Greek alphabet

Very large numbers are expressed in powers of 10. For instance, the mass of the Sun is 2×10^{30} kg (expressed as two times 10 to the 30 kilograms), which is the exact equivalent of writing 2 followed by 30 zeros. Powers that have negative numbers are expressed as 'per', for example, km·s^{-1} is kilometres per second, and cm^{-3} is per cubic centimetre.

Angular measurements
1° (degree) = 1/360th part of a circle
1' (arc minute) = 1/60th of a degree
1" (arc second) = 1/60th of an arc minute
The Moon is 0.5° in diameter (dia.).

Distance measurements
1 astronomical unit (AU)
  = 149 597 870 km
  = 149.6×10^6 km
1 light year = distance travelled by light in one year
  = 9.4607×10^{12} km
  = 63 240 AU
1 parsec (pc) = 3.0857×10^{13} km
  = 3.2616 l.y.
1 kpc = 1 000 pc (kiloparsec)
1 Mpc = 1 000 kpc (Megaparsec)

Temperature
0 °C = zero degrees Centigrade, freezing point of water
100 °C = boiling point of water
1 K = 1 degree Kelvin = -272 °C

Greek alphabet
Normally the brightest star in a constellation is called Alpha, the second brightest Beta, and so on.

α	alpha	ν	nu
β	beta	ξ	xi
γ	gamma	ο	omicron
δ	delta	π	pi
ε	epsilon	ρ	ro
ζ	zeta	σ	sigma
η	eta	τ	tau
θ	theta	υ	upsilon
ι	iota	φ	phi
κ	kappa	χ	chi
λ	lambda	ψ	psi
μ	mu	ω	omega

The bright star Theta Orionis is actually a five-star system called the Trapezium Cluster, at the heart of the Orion Nebula (M42). All of the stars were born together out of the gas that is now illuminated by these hot young stars. The gas and cluster can easily be seen through binoculars or a small telescope. (NASA/ESA)

APPENDIX 2: The constellations

The names of the 88 constellations are presented together with the official IAU three-letter abbreviations. The constellations appearing in **bold type** are circumpolar as seen from southern Africa; those in *italics* are too far north and can never be seen from these latitudes.

Depending on your exact latitude, some of the constellations marked as circumpolar may in fact set, and some marked as never rising may just rise above the far northern horizon.

Constellation	Abbr.	English description
Andromeda	And	Daughter of Cepheus
Antlia	Ant	Air pump
Apus	**Aps**	**Bird of paradise**
Aquarius	Aqr	Water bearer
Aquila	Aql	Eagle
Ara	Ara	Altar
Aries	Ari	Ram
Auriger	Aur	Charioteer or wagoner
Bootes	Boo	Bear hunter
Caelum	Cae	Sculptor's chisel
Camelopardalis	*Cam*	*Giraffe*
Cancer	Cnc	Crab
Canes Venatici	CVn	Hunting dogs
Canis Major	CMa	Greater dog
Canis Minor	CMi	Lesser dog
Capricornus	Cap	Goat
Carina	Car	Keel
Cassiopeia	*Cas*	*Queen Cassiopeia*
Centaurus	Cen	Centaur
Cepheus	*Cep*	*Cepheus*
Cetus	Cet	Sea monster
Chamaeleon	**Cha**	**Chameleon**
Circinus	**Cir**	**Pair of compasses**
Columba	Col	Noah's dove
Coma Berenices	Com	Berenice's hair
Corona Australis	CrA	Southern crown
Corona Borealis	CrB	Northern crown
Corvus	Crv	Crow
Crater	Crt	Cup
Crux	**Cru**	**Southern Cross**
Cygnus	Cyg	Swan
Delphinus	Del	Dolphin
Dorado	**Dor**	**Goldfish or swordfish**
Draco	*Dra*	*Dragon*
Equuleus	Equ	Foal
Eridanus	Eri	River
Fornax	For	Chemical furnace
Gemini	Gem	Twins
Grus	Gru	Crane
Hercules	Her	Hercules
Horologium	Hor	Pendulum clock
Hydra	Hya	Water serpent
Hydrus	**Hyi**	**Water snake**
Indus	Ind	American Indian
Lacerta	Lac	Lizard
Leo	Leo	Lion
Leo Minor	LMi	Lesser lion (cub)
Lepus	Lep	Hare
Libra	Lib	Balance or scales
Lupus	Lup	Wolf
Lynx	Lyn	Lynx or tiger
Lyra	Lyr	Lyre or harp
Mensa	**Men**	**Table Mountain**
Microscopium	Mic	Microscope
Monoceros	Mon	Unicorn
Musca	**Mus**	**Fly**
Norma	Nor	Carpenter's square
Octans	**Oct**	**Octant**
Ophiuchus	Oph	Serpent holder
Orion	Ori	Hunter
Pavo	**Pav**	**Peacock**
Pegasus	Peg	Winged horse
Perseus	Per	Perseus, the Champion
Phoenix	Phe	Mythical bird
Pictor	Pic	Painter's easel
Pisces	Psc	Fishes
Piscis Austrinus	PsA	Southern fish
Puppis	Pup	Stern
Pyxis	Pyx	Compass box
Reticulum	Ret	Net
Sagitta	Sge	Arrow
Sagittarius	Sgr	Archer
Scorpius	Sco	Scorpion
Sculptor	Scl	Sculptor's studio
Scutum	Sct	Shield
Serpens	Ser	Serpent
Sextans	Sex	Sextant
Taurus	Tau	Bull
Telescopium	Tel	Telescope
Triangulum	Tri	Triangle
Triangulum Australe	**TrA**	**Southern triangle**
Tucana	Tuc	Toucan
Ursa Major	*UMa*	*Greater bear*
Ursa Minor	*UMi*	*Lesser bear*
Vela	Vel	Ship's sail
Virgo	Vir	Virgin
Volans	**Vol**	**Flying fish**
Vulpecula	Vul	Fox

APPENDIX 3: Data for the 30 brightest stars

The brightest star in the sky is the Sun, with an apparent magnitude of -26.7 and spectral class G2. By definition it lies at a mean distance of 1 astronomical unit or 4.85×10^{-6} pc.

	Star	Proper name	App. mg.	Spectral type	Distance (pc)	Notes
1	α CMa	Sirius	−1.46	A1V	2.7	Double
2	α Car	Canopus	−0.72	F0 II	40	
3	α Cen	Rigel Kentaurus	−0.27	G2V	1.3	Triple
4	α Boo	Arcturus	−0.04	K2III	11	
5	α Lyr	Vega	0.03	A0 V	8.1	
6	α Aur	Capella	0.08	G8 III	14	See note*
7	β Ori	Rigel	0.12	B8 Ia	250	
8	α Cmi	Procyon	0.38	F5 IV-V	3.5	
9	α Eri	Achernar	0.46	B3 Vp	39	
10	β Cen	Hadar	0.61	B1 III	120	
11	α Aql	Altair	0.77	A7 IV-V	5.0	
12	α Ori	Betelgeuse	0.80	M2 Ia-Iab	200	Variable
13	α Tau	Aldebaran	0.85	K5 III	21	
14	α Cru	Acrux	0.87	B1 IV	80	Double
15	α Sco	Antares	0.96	M1 Ib	160	Slightly var.
16	α Vir	Spica	1.00	B1 V	84	
17	β Gem	Pollux	1.14	K0 III	11	
18	α PsA	Formalhaut	1.16	A3 V	7.1	
19	α Cyg	Deneb	1.25	A2 Ia	490	
20	β Cru	Mimosa	1.28	B0 IV	150	Slightly var.
21	α Leo	Regulus	1.35	B7 V	26	Faint triplet
22	ε Cma	Adhara	1.50	B2 II	208	Double
23	α Gem	Castor	1.59	A1 V	14	Slightly var.
24	λ Sco	Shaula	1.63	B1 IV	310	
25	γ Cru	Gamma Crucis	1.63	M4 IIIb	68	
26	γ Ori	Bellatrix	1.64	B2 III	144	
27	β Tau	El Nath	1.65	B7 III	92	
28	β Car	Miaplacidus	1.68	A1 III	26	
29	ε Ori	Alnilam	1.70	B0 Ia	490	
30	α Gru	Al Na'ir	1.74	B7 IV	20	

* Although Capella appears to be a single star to the unaided eye, it is actually a system of four stars in two binary pairs. If they were to be separated both Alpha Capella (α Aur) and Beta Capella (β Aur) would rank in the top 10 brightest stars.

OPPOSITE: *Abell 1689 comprises a massive cluster of galaxies, seen as yellowish objects in this Hubble Space Telescope image. The gravity of clusters of trillions of stars along with dark matter causes a distortion in space called a gravitational lens. Light from far more distant galaxies is distorted into arcs.* (NASA/JPL/Caltech)

APPENDIX 4: Planetary data

Planet	Mean distance from Sun (AU)	Sidereal period (years)	Synodic period (days)	Axial rotation period * (days)	Opposition diameter (")	Equator diameter (km)
Mercury	0.387	0.241	115.88	58.79	7.8	4 879
Venus	0.723	0.615	583.92	-243.0	25.2	12 104
Earth	1.000	1.001		0.997		12 756
Mars	1.524	1.881	779.94	1.026	17.8	6 792
Jupiter	5.204	11.862	398.88	0.414	46.8	142 984
Saturn	9.582	29.458	378.09	0.445	19.4	120 536
Uranus	19.201	84.011	369.66	-0.718	3.8	51 118
Neptune	30.047	164.79	367.49	0.673	2.4	49 528

Notes
* Minus sign indicates retrograde direction   ** Magnitudes at opposition or, for Mercury and Venus, at greatest elongation

GLOSSARY

Aphelion Point in the orbital path of a body that is furthest from the Sun.

Astronomical unit The mean Sun–Earth distance, equal to 149 597 870 km. Abbreviation: AU.

Big bang A cosmological theory that the universe originated about 1.4×10^{10} years ago (the exact age depends on the Hubble constant), when all matter was contained in a very small volume at a very high temperature. Evidence to support this theory includes the expansion of the universe as measured by the redshifts of galaxies and the 3 °K microwave background radiation, which suggests that the universe must have been much hotter in the past.

Black hole An object whose gravitational attraction is so great that nothing, not even light, can escape from it. Black holes can only be detected by their gravitational influence on other bodies. The constellation of Cygnus contains a very bright X-ray source, Cygnus X-1, thought to be a black hole.

Celestial sphere An imaginary sphere onto which are drawn celestial bodies and other points in the sky as seen from Earth. The key reference points are the celestial poles, equator, ecliptic, horizon and zenith.

Cepheid variable A very luminous yellow pulsating super-giant star that varies in brightness (by, typically, 1 mag) with a period of 1 to 100 days. A relationship between the period and luminosity enables distances to be measured.

Circumpolar Describes those constellations and stars that never disappear below the horizon as seen from the observer's latitude.

Mass (Earth = 1)	Density (water = 1)	Magnitude** (opposition)	Orbital eccentricity	Orbital inclination (degrees)	Number of satellites	Ring system
0.055	5.427	+0.00	0.2056	7.00	0	No
0.815	5.243	–4.4	0.0067	3.39	0	No
1.000	5.515		0.0167	0.00	1	No
0.107	3.933	–2.0	0.0935	25.19	1	No
317.83	1.326	–2.3	0.0489	1.30	63	Yes
95.159	0.687	+0.7	0.0565	2.49	62	Yes
14.536	1.270	+5.5	0.0457	0.77	27	Yes
17.147	1.638	+7.8	0.0113	1.77	13	Yes

Comet A minor member of the solar system composed of a nucleus made of dust, frozen water vapour and gases. As the comet nears the Sun it develops a coma and possibly a tail. Only 4% of the known comets are periodic or returning. All comets move in highly elliptical orbits.

Conjunction The point in the orbit of a body that is on the far side of, and in line with, the Sun as seen from Earth. In the case of Mercury and Venus this point is referred to as 'inferior conjunction', and when the planet lies between the Sun and the Earth, it reaches 'superior conjunction'.

Constellation One of 88 areas into which the sky is divided, based on groups of stars considered to depict various mythological creatures or instruments, etc. There is no physical meaning to the patterns.

Declination Lines drawn on the celestial sphere equivalent to lines of latitude on Earth.

Eclipse A solar eclipse occurs when the Moon lies between the Sun and the Earth, and a lunar eclipse when the Earth is between the Moon and the Sun. Up to seven eclipses can occur in one year, either five solar and two lunar, or four solar and three lunar. Total eclipses of the Sun from any one place are very rare, occurring, on average, once every 360 years.

Ecliptic The path on the celestial sphere traced out by the Sun (and that the planets closely follow). It is inclined at approximately 23.43° to the equator, the tilt angle of the Earth's rotation axis.

Elongation The angular distance of Mercury or Venus from the Sun.

Equinoxes The Sun crosses the equator from south to north on about 21 March and from north to south near 23 September each year. These points on the ecliptic are known as the 'vernal equinox' and 'autumnal equinox' respectively. On these dates the northern and southern hemispheres experience an equal amount of day and night.

Faculae (singular: **facula**) Bright white spots on the solar disc, several thousands of kilometres in size. These are convection cells that form and dissipate over a timescale of several minutes, and they are associated with magnetic field lines.

Galaxy A very large collection of stars and interstellar material. Galaxies are the fundamental building block of the universe. They are classified into spirals, ellipticals, lenticulars and irregulars. Most galaxies are not isolated but occur in pairs or larger groups. Our own galaxy, called the Milky Way, or the Galaxy, is 30 kpc in diameter and contains at least 5×10^{11} solar masses.

Hubble's law The velocity of recession of a galaxy (measured by its redshift) is linearly proportional to its distance from us. Thus, the further away a galaxy is, the faster it appears to be moving. The velocity is given by the equation $V = H_0 \times$ distance, where H_0 is Hubble's constant, currently set at 73.5 ± 3.2 km·s^{-1}·Mpc^{-1}.

Interstellar medium The material between the stars that accounts for at least 10% of the mass of a typical spiral galaxy and comprises primarily hydrogen, helium, oxygen, nitrogen, heavier elements and dust.

Light year The distance travelled by light in one year, 9.4607×10^{12} km.

Local Group A collection of about 30 galaxies, including our own Milky Way, which form a distinct unit.

Magellanic Clouds Two external galaxies that are satellites to our own galaxy. The Large Magellanic Cloud (LMC) lies in the constellation of Dorado and the Small Magellanic Cloud (SMC) in Tucana. They are two of the nearest galaxies to us at 54.8 kpc (LMC) and 64.3 kpc (SMC).

Magnitude A logarithmic measure of the brightness of a star or other celestial object, such that a difference of five magnitudes is equivalent to a difference in brightness of 100. The brightest stars are magnitude -1, the faintest seen by the eye magnitude 6. Apparent magnitudes give no indication of a star's true brightness. Absolute magnitudes are used for such comparisons. It is the magnitude the object would have if it were placed at a standard distance of 10 pc. Abbreviation: mag.

Meridian A line connecting the celestial poles and the zenith.

Milky Way A faint band of light crossing the sky (roughly from north to south) that is composed of tens of thousands of stars and other objects. It is our own Galaxy.

Nebulae (singular: **nebula**) Regions of dust and gas in the interstellar medium that appear as 'nebulous patches' in a small telescope. Nebulae can be areas of stellar birth, or may be formed by the death of a star.

Neutron star A very dense star formed by a supernova explosion. These stars are typically only a few tens of kilometres in diameter, yet they have the same mass as the Sun.

Novae (singular: **nova**) A star that suddenly increases in brightness by 10 magnitudes or more (a factor of 10 000 in brightness). About 10 to 15 are seen in our Galaxy each year. Novae are stars that form part of a close binary system, one component being a white dwarf. Novae are thought to recur approximately once every 10 000 years.

Opposition The point in the orbit of a body when it is opposite the Sun in the sky as seen from Earth, is thus visible all night and is usually near maximum brightness.

Parsec Derived from 'parallax-second', it refers to the distance at which one astronomical unit subtends an angle of one second of arc. It is used for distances beyond the solar system. Abbreviation: pc; 1 000 pc = 1 kpc and 1 000 kpc = 1 Mpc.

Perihelion The point in the orbital path of a body that is closest to the Sun.

Precession The rotation axis of the Earth describes a cone like a spinning top that is just about to topple. It takes 25 800 years or over 9 million revolutions to make one circuit. As a result, the co-ordinates of stars marked on the celestial sphere change very slowly.

Pulsar A rapidly rotating neutron star that is analogous to a lighthouse, 'pulsing' out radiation to the observer as it turns around. Originally discovered at radio wavelengths, two have now been detected in visible light. The most famous example is the Crab Pulsar that was created in the supernova explosion of AD 1054.

Quasar The nucleus of an extremely bright galaxy. Quasars are also called quasi-stellar objects or QSOs because they are so remote that they look almost like point sources. These extragalactic compact objects emit more energy than 100 normal galaxies! Their tremendous luminosity allows them to be seen at great distances, and so they have very large redshifts. Quasars are the most remote objects known.

Red giant A star that has reached its final stages of life, and is now burning helium in its core and hydrogen in an outer shell. Its surface temperature is only 3 000 °C and its diameter several hundred times that of the Sun.

Redshift The displacement of spectral features towards longer ('redder') wavelengths caused by the movement of an object away from us. The faster it is receding, the greater the redshift. Some nearby objects are moving towards us and are said to be blueshifted.

Retrograde motion The opposite of the normal or pro-grade motion. The apparent motion of the superior planets across the sky as seen from Earth is normally from east to west. However, this motion can appear to be reversed because of the Earth's motion around the Sun. Mars has a very pronounced retrograde motion. The term also applies to the axial tilt of planets. If the tilt exceeds 90° the body spins backwards and is said to be in retrograde motion.

Right ascension The equivalent of lines of longitude drawn on the celestial sphere, measured eastwards from the vernal equinox to the object. Usually expressed in hours, minutes and seconds rather than degrees, there being 24 hours in one revolution.

RR Lyrae variables Very short-period variables with an absolute magnitude of + 0.5, used as a distance indicator – especially to globular clusters.

Separation The angular distance between two objects, for instance stars, measured in arc seconds, arc minutes or degrees.

Sidereal period The time taken for a body to make one complete circuit around the celestial sphere as seen from the Sun.

Solar system All of the objects that are held by the gravitational field of the Sun, including the planets and their satellites, asteroids, comets, and interplanetary dust. The solar system extends about a quarter of the way to the nearest star, which is where comets are thought to originate.

Spectral class A method of grouping stars according to the appearance of their spectra, which is related to their temperature. The different classes are O, B, A, F, G, K, M, R, N, S, with O and B stars being very hot and blue, and M stars very cool and red.

Sun Our nearest star. It is the only one that can be seen as a disc, since the others are so far away. It is a typical middle-aged star that shines by converting hydrogen into helium.

Supernova A stellar explosion of titanic proportions in which all of the outer layers of a star are blown away at very high velocities of up to 30 000 km·s^{-1}. The stellar core spins rapidly to conserve angular momentum, and it turns into a neutron star. Supernova can outshine an entire galaxy as they emit as much energy in a few days as the Sun does in its entire lifetime. The expanding shell of debris, called a 'supernova remnant', forms a nebula.

Synodic period The time interval between successive oppositions of a body as seen from Earth.

Transit The passage of one (usually) small body in front of another – for example Mercury and Venus across the disc of the Sun. It is also used to describe a star or other object when it lies on the north–south line (meridian) of the celestial sphere.

Universe The total sum of everything that exists, including space, time, matter and energy.

Variable star A star that varies in brightness in either a regular or irregular fashion. Variables are important as distance indicators in the Local Group of galaxies.

Vernal equinox The point on the celestial sphere where the Sun crosses the equator from south to north, and from which right ascension is measured.

White dwarf A very dense compact star with the same volume as the Earth and the same mass as the Sun. A thimbleful of this material would weigh over 10 tonnes. These objects are of low luminosity and so are very faint. They may be the graveyards of normal stars with masses less than 1.4 times that of the Sun. They also occur in binary systems associated with novae.

Zodiacal light A faint glow of light extending away from the Sun in a conical shape and that lies in the plane of the ecliptic. It is caused by the reflection of light off interplanetary dust.

The Sagittarius (southern winter) region of the Milky Way. North is at the top. The galactic plane contains numerous clusters and lots of dust and gas. To the south the Large and Small Magellanic Clouds are clearly visible. The Sagittarius area is rich in nebula and star clusters and provides hours of observing fun, even with binoculars. This spectacular sight is not available to the northern hemisphere observer.
(Axel Mellinger, Central Michigan University, 2009)

The Orion arm of the Milky Way dominates the southern summer sky. It is clearly not as rich as the galactic centre and there is less dust and gas. Don't expect to see this much detail, especially from a light-polluted sky. The field of view here is a full 360 degrees. See whether you can identify constellations by matching this image to some of the star charts.
(Axel Mellinger, Central Michigan University, 2009)

RESOURCES LIST

The Astronomical Society of Southern Africa (http://assa.saao.ac.za/) caters for both the complete novice and the professional astronomer. Membership is open to anyone with an interest in astronomy. Members may subscribe to the monthly American magazine *Sky & Telescope* at a significantly discounted rate. There are seven local centres that hold regular meetings and observing parties. Joining an astronomical society is one of the best ways to learn more about the subject.

The society's own annual publication, *Sky Guide Africa South – Astronomical Handbook for Southern Africa*, gives detailed information and astronomical events for the current year and is highly recommended.

The internet has almost unlimited information on astronomy. Enter these expressions in a search engine to find the following useful websites:

Astronomy Picture of the Day	apod.nasa.gov
Desktop planetarium	http://www.stellarium.org/
Sky and Telescope	http://www.skyandtelescope.com/
South African Observatory	http://www.saao.ac.za/
Private observatories South Africa	http://assa.saao.ac.za/html/privateamateursa.html

If you have a Smart Phone there are interactive applications that provide real-time star charts to identify objects as you move the device around the sky.

FURTHER READING

Fairall, A. 2002. *Cape Town Planetarium's Starwatching: A Southern Hemisphere Guide to the Galaxy*. Random House Struik, Cape Town.

Fairall, A. 2008. *Starwise: A Beginner's Guide to the Universe*. Random House Struik, Cape Town.

Hawking, S. & Mlodinow, L. 2011. *The Grand Design*. Bantam Books, New York.

Heifetz, M. & Tirion, W. 2007. *A Walk Through the Southern Sky: A Guide to Stars and Constellations and their Legends*. Cambridge University Press, Cape Town.

INDEX

Bold numbers indicate illustrations/tables

A

Acrux 94, **100**
Aldebaran **76, 77**, 94, 96, **100**
Algol 96
Alpha Centauri 11, 59, 61, 93
Alpha Leonis 95
Altair **80, 81, 82, 83, 100**
Andromeda 68, **80, 81**, 92
Andromeda Galaxy (Nebula) 10, 61, 67, 68, **68–69**, **80–81**, **86, 87**, 92
Antares 96, **100**
aphelion 34, 47, 102
Aquarius 92, **99**
Aquila 92, **99**
Ara 92, 94, **99**
Arcturus **78, 79**, 92, **100**
Ariel 42, **42**
ascension 7, 75, 107
  lines of right **8**, 9, 105
asteroid belt 19, 50–51, 53
asteroids 18, 35, **50**, 51, 106
Astraea 51
astronomical distances 10–11, **10**, 12
astronomical photography 17
Astronomical Society of SA 108
astronomical units (AU) 10, 28, 98, 100, 102, 105
Auriga 92
aurorae 55, **55**
  australis 55, **55**
  borealis 55

B

Baily's beads 33
Beehive open cluster 92
Belinda **42**
Bessel's star 12
Beta Centauri 93
Beta Lyrae 61, **66**
Beta Perseus 96
Betelgeuse 75, 96, **100**
'big bang' 72, 73, 102

binoculars 14–15, 17, 21, **21**
black holes 56, 63, **63**, 71, 97, 102
blueshift 60, 105
Bootes **78, 79**, 92, **99**

C

Callisto 37, **37**
cameras (CCD) 5, 15, 17, 71, 75
Cancer 92, **99**
Canes Venatici 92, **99**
Canis Major 4, 93, **99**
Canis Minor 4, 93, **99**
Canopus 93, **100**
Capella 92, **100**
Capricornus 44, 93, **99**
carbon dioxide 27, 29, **34**, 35, **37**
Carina 93, 95, 97, **99**
Castor 59, 94
celestial sphere 7–9, 102, 103, 105, 107
Centaurus 69, 93, 94, **99**
Cepheids 12, **59**, 61, 68, 92, 102
Ceres 19, **46**, 50, 51
Cetus 94
Charon 30, 47, **47**
Coal Sack 66, 94
Coma 69
Coma Cluster **10**, 69
comets 5, 10, 18, 19, 36, 51–53, 54, 64, 103, 106
  coma 10, 52
  long-period 52
  nucleus 52
  short-period 52
  tail 52
Cone Nebula 66, 95
conjuction 103
  inferior 22, **22**, 26
  superior 22, **22**
constellations 4, 6–7, **6**, 8, 9, 37, 44, **53**, 54, 54, 59, **65**, 68, 69, 75, 92, 93, 95, 96, 97, 99, 102, 103, 104
corona 33, **33**
Corona Australis **99**

Corona Borealis **78, 79, 99**
Corvus 94, **99**
Crab Nebula 64, 65, 97
Cressida **42**
Crux 94, **100**
Cygnus **80, 81, 99**, 102

D

'dark energy' 73, **73**
declination **7**, 9, 40, 75, 103
  lines of 8
Degas (crater) **24**
Deimos 35
Delphinus 96, **99**
Delta Cephei 61, 92
Delta Orionis 66
Deneb **80, 81, 82, 83, 100**
Desdemona **42**
Despina 44
Dione **40**
Dorado 94, **99**, 104
double stars 59–60, 93, 94
Dumbbell Nebula 97
dust 18, 32, 35, 38, 42, **42**, 47, 52, **54**, 55, 56, 62, 64, 66, 70, 103, 104, 106
dwarf planets 10, **10**, 18, 19, 46, **47**, 48, **48**, 49, **49**, 50, 51
Dysnomia 48, **48**

E

Earth 4, 7, **7**, 8, **8**, 9. **9**, 10, **10**, 11, 12, 13, **13**, 16, **18**, 19, **19**, 20, 22, **22**, 23, 24, 25, **25**, 26, 27, 28–29, **28**, 30, 32, **32**, 33, 34, 35, 36, **36**, 37, 37, 38, **38**, 40, 42, 43, 44, 45, **46**, 47, **50**, 51, 53, 54, 55, 57, 59, 60, 61, 63, 64, 66, **67**, 74, 103, 104, 105, 106
  age 29
  atmosphere 28
  axis of rotation 7, 9, 16, 97
  equator 7, 8, **8**, 9, 19, 21, 33
eclipses 5, 32–33, **32, 33**, 37, 47, 60, **60**, 61, 103
  Algol-type **60**, 61

annular 33, **33**
'diamond ring' **33**
ecliptic 4, 8, 9, **23**, 24, 32, 34, 36, 40, 42, 43, 47, 51, 54, **54**, 74, 75, 78, 82, 92, 93, 96, 102, 103, 106
electromagnetic spectrum 13, **13**
elongation 22, **22**, 24, 26, 103
Enceladus **40**
energy 20, 36, 41, 60, 63, 65, 105, 106
Enif 96
Epsilon Piscium 96
equinoxes 8, **8**, 9, **9**, 12, 103, 104, 105, 106
Eris 19, **46**, 48, **48**
Eros 18
Eta Carina 93, 95
Europa 37, **37**, 38, **39**
eyes 11, 13, 14, 15
    dark adaptation 14

F

faculae **21**, 104
False Cross **90**, **91**, 93, 97
fireballs **53**, 54
Fornax **69**, 94, **99**

G

galactic centre **82**, **83**, **88**, **89**
Galatea 44
galaxies 5, **6**, 10, **10**, 12, 29, 39, 61, 63, 64, 65, 67, **67**, 68, 69, 72, **72**, 73, 75, 92, 94, 95, 96, 104, 105, 106
    barred spiral 70, 94
    classification 70–71
    dwarf elliptical 70
    elliptical 68, 70
    irregular **67**, 70, 71, 94
    lenticular 70
    morphology 70, **70**
    nucleus 71
    radio **67**
    spiral **10**, 70, **71**, 73, 92, 94, 95
Gamma Lyrae 66
Ganymede 37, **37**, 38, **38**, 39
gas 20, 52, **52**, 56, 57, 62, 64, 65, 66, 70, 103, 104
gas giants **19**, 36, **36**, **43**, 44

gegenschein 55
Gemini 9, 59, 94, **99**
globular clusters **6**, 56, 61, 66, 67, **67**, 68, **71**, 75, 80, 86, 92, 93, 94, 95, 96, 97, 106
gravitation 9, 9, 18, 36, 41, 46, 62, 63, 103
gravitational lens 73, 100
Grus 94, **99**

H

Hadar **90**, **91**, 93, **100**
Halley's comet **51**, 52, 54
Haumea 19, **46**, 48–49, **48**
helium 20, 36, 40, 41, 43, **43**, 61, 62, 63, 64, 104, 105, 106
hemispheres 6, 8, **16**, 24, 34, 34, 40, **41**, 55, **66**, 74, 75, 92, 93, 95, 96, 97, 104
Hercules 66, 94, **99**
Hertzsprung-Russell (H-R) diagram 59, **59**
Hi'iaka **48**, 49
Hickson Compact Group **72**
Hipparcos satellite 12, **12**
Hoba meteorite 53
horizon 24, 53, 54, 61, 78, 82, 86, 90, 99, 102
Horsehead Nebula 66
Hubble's law 12, 72, 104
Hubble's Variable Nebula 95
Hyades 66, **76**, **77**, 97
Hydra 47, **47**, 95, **99**
hydrogen 20, 36, 40, 41, 43, **43**, 62, 63, 64, 65, 66, 104, 105, 106

I

ice ages 21, 60
interplanetary matter 18, 64
interstellar matter (medium) 56, 62, 64, 104
Io 37, **37**, 38, **38**

J

Jewel Box **67**, 94
Juno 36, 50
Jupiter 10, **18**, 19, 36–39, **36**, **38**, 40, 43, **47**, 50, **50**, **102**
    Great Red Spot **36**, 37
    ring system 38
    rotation 38, 39

synodic period 36
water 36

K

Kappa Crucis 66, **67**, 94
Kepler's laws **23**, 33
Keyhole Nebula 93
Kuiper Belt 46, 49

L

Lagoon Nebula 96
Larissa 44
latitude 7, **7**, 8, 9, 33, 37, 55, 103
Leo **53**, **78**, **79**, 95, **99**
Lepus 4, **99**
Libra 95, **99**
life 20, 27, 28, 29
light pollution 55, 75
light years 10–11, 13, 73, 92, 98, 104
Local Group 68, **69**, 96, 97, 104, 106
longitude 7, **7**, 8, 9, 75, 105
luminosity 12, 20, 29, 58, **59**, 61, 62, 63, 66, 68, 71, 102, 105, 106
Lyra 65, 95, **99**

M

Magellanic clouds **54**, **61**, 104
    Large 6, **6**, 65, 68, 71, **88**, **89**, **90**, **91**, 94, 104
    Small **6**, 61, 66, 68, **88**, **89**, **90**, **91**, 97, 104
magnetic fields 20, 25, 44, 51, 104
magnification **14**, 15, **21**, 65
magnitude 13, 58, **59**, 61, 92, 104
Makemake 19, **46**, 49, **49**
Mars 10, 10, 18, **18**, 19, 22, 23, **23**, 29, 34–35, **35**, **50**, 51, **78**, **79**, 96, **102**, 105
    atmosphere 29, 35
    orbit 34
    rotation 35
    seasons 34, 35
    Syrtis Major hemisphere **34**, 35
    Valles Marineris

hemisphere 34
water 35
Mbozi meteorite 53
McNaught 2006 P1 Comet 52
Mensa 6, **6**, **99**
Mercury 10, **18**, 19, 22, 24–25, **24**, **25**, 26, 34, 38, 41, **50**, 51, **102**, 103, 106
   atmosphere 25, **25**
   temperatures 25
   transits 24, 25, **25**
Messier catalogue 64, 75, 92
meteor showers **53**, 54, 92
meteorites 38, 53
meteors 18, 25, 53–54, 64, 92
methane 36, 40, 41, 42, 43, **43**, 45, 47, 49
Milk Dipper 96
Milky Way **4**, **6**, 17, 55, **67**, 75, **76**, **77**, 80, **81**, **84**, **85**, **86**, **87**, 92, 93, 94, 95, 96, 104, **107**
Milky Way Galaxy 10, **10**, 12, 54, 56, **57**, 64, 68, **69**, 70, 96
   nucleus 56
   spiral arms 56, **57**, 64
Mimas **40**
Mira 12, 61, 62, **62**, 94
Miranda 42
Monoceros 66, 95, 99
Moon 4, 9, 10, **10**, 12, 13, 16, 22, 25, 26, 29, 30, **30**, **31**, 32, 33, **33**, 47, 75, 92, 103
   craters 54
   phases 30
   water 30
moons (natural satellites) 5, 18, 19, 35, 37, **37**, 38, **38**, 39, 41, 42, **42**, 43, 44, **45**, 46, **46**, 47, 48, **48**, 49

N

Naiad 44
Namaka **48**, 49
nebulae 64–66, 92, 95, 97, 104
   dark 64, 66, 92, 94
   diffuse 75
   emission 64
   planetary 64, 65, **65**, 75
   reflection 64
   supernova remnants 64, 65

Neptune 10, 19, **19**, 41, 42, 43–45, **43**, **44**, **45**, 46, 47, 65, **102**
   orbit 43
   rings **44**, 45
Nereid 44
neutron stars 63, **63**, 65, 104, 105, 106
nitrogen 41, 45, 47, 49, 55, 104
Nix 47, **47**
Nix Olympica 35
Norma Cluster 69
novae 105, 106
nuclear reactions 20, 62, 63

O

Oberon 42
occultation 32, 37
Omega Centauri 66, **67**, 94, 97
Omega Nebula 96
Omega Ursae Majoris 61
Omicron Ceti 62, **62**
Oort Cloud 45, 53
Ophiuchus 95, 96, **99**
opposition 22, **22**, **23**, 35, 36, 37, 40, 42, 49, 96, **102**, **103**, 105, 106
orbits 8, 9, 11, **11**, 12, 18, 19, 22, **22**, 23, **23**, 24, 25, **25**, 27, 28, 29, 32, 34, 35, 36, 37, **37**, 38, 39, **39**, 40, **41**, 42, 43, 44, 46, 47, **48**, 49, 50, **50**, 51, 52, 56, 59, 60, **62**, 64, 103
Orion 4, **53**, 56, 64, 66, 75, **76**, **77**, **84**, **85**, 94, 95, 96, **98**, **107**
   belt 95
   Great Nebula 64, 95
Orion Nebula 64, **76**, **77**, **98**
oxygen 55, 64, 104

P

P4 23, **23**, 47, **47**
Pallas 50
parallax 11, **11**, 12, **12**, 93, 105
parsecs 11, 12, 56, 66, 68, 69, 73, 98, 105
Pavo 95, **99**
Pegasus 75, **80**, **81**, 95, 96, **99**
penumbra 32, **32**
perihelion 34, 36, 47, 52, 105
Perseus 69, 96, **99**

Phobos 35
Pinwheel 97
Pisces 8, 69, 96, **99**
planetary motions 22, 23
planetary nebulae 29, 63, **65**, 75, 92, 95, 97
planetary positions 22, **22**
planets 4, 5, 9, 10, **10**, 13, 16, 18, **18–19**, 22, **22**, 23, **23**, 24, 25, **25**, 26, 28, 29, 30, 34, 35, **35**, 36, 37, **37**, **38**, 39, 40, 41, **41**, 42, **42**, 43, **43**, 44, **44**, 45, 46, **46**, 47, **47**, 51, 52, 54, 55, 64, 68, 72, 78, **102–103**, 105, 106
Pleiades 64, 66, **76**, **77**, **84**, **85**, 97
Pluto 10, **10**, 19, 30, **38**, 46, **46**, 47, **47**, **48**, **48**, 49
plutoids 19, 46, **46**, 49, 50
Pointers 93
Polaris **9**, 92
poles 7, 8, 20, 30, **34**, 40, 55, 90, 102, 104
Pollux 94, **100**
Portia 42
Praesepe open cluster 92
precession 8, 9, **9**, 12, 105
Procyon 93, **100**
Proteus 44
Proxima Centauri 10, **10**, 11, 59, 93
Puck **42**
pulsars 63, 65, **67**, 97, 105
'Puppis' 93, **99**
Pwyll (crater) **39**
'Pyxis' 93, **99**

Q

quadrature 22, **22**
quasars 71, 105

R

R Monocerotis 95
red giants 12, 29, 59, 62, **62**, 63, 66, 92, 96, 105
redshift 12, 60, 73, 97, **102**, 104, 105
Regulus **78**, **79**, 95, **100**
Reticulum **6**, **99**
Rhea **40**
Rigel Kentaurus 75, **90**, **91**, 93, **100**

INDEX   111

Ring Nebula 65, 95
Ringtail Galaxy 94
Rosette Nebula 95
RR Lyrae 59, 59, 61, 92, 97, 106

S

Sagittarius 9, 56, 64, 65, 66, 75, 96, **99**, **107**
Saturn 10, 10, **18**, 19, **23**, 38, 40–41, **40**, **41**, 42, 43, **78**, **79**, 92, **102**
   atmosphere 40
   rings 40, 41
   sideral period 40
   synodic period 40
Scorpius 75, 96, **99**
Sculptor 96, **99**
Scutum **80**, **81**, **99**
seasons **9**, 22, 34, 35
Serpens **80**, **81**, 95, 96, **99**
Serpens Caput 96
Serpens Cauda 96
Seven Sisters 64, 97
Seyfert galaxies 71, **71**
Ship 93, **99**
Sirius 9, 93, **100**
sodium **58**, 64
solar eclipses 5, 32, 33
solar system 10, **10**, 18–19, 20, 23, 24, 25, 29, 30, 36, **37**, **38**, 40, 41, 43, 45, 46, 47, 48, 49, 50, 51, 53, 54, 57, 59, 66, 103, 105, 106
Sombrero (spiral) 97
Southern Cross 66, **84**, **85**, **88**, **89**, **90**, **91**, 93, **99**
Spica **78**, **79**, **100**
star charts 7, 8, 9, 64, 74–91, 108
star clusters 64, 66–67, 92, 93, 96, 97
stars **4**, **4**, 6, **6**, 9, 11, 12, 13, 17, 18, 22, 23, 24, 28, 29, 30, 32, 37, 44, 45, 47, 51, 52, 56, 58–59, **63**, 64, 65, 66, **67**, 68, 69, 72, 73, 74, 92, 93, 94, 96, 97, 100, 102, 103, 104, 105, 106
   binary 60
   contact binary 61

evolution 62–63
expansion 62
luminosity 58, **58**
pulsations 61
spectra 58, **58**
temperatures 58, **58**
variable 60–62, 68, 94, 100, 106
sulphuric acid **26**, 27
Sun 4, 5, **8**, 9, **9**, 10, **10**, 11, 13, 18, **18**, 19, 20–21, 22, **22**, 23, **23**, 25, **25**, 26, 28, 29, 30, 32, 33, 34, 36, 37, 38, 40, 41, 42, 43, 46, 47, 48, **50**, 51, 52, 53, 55, 56, **57**, 58, 59, 61, 62, 63, 66, 71, 74, 75, 93, 94, 97, 100, 102, 103, 104, 105, 106
sunspots 20, **20**, 21, **21**, 25
supernovae 5, 63, 64, 65, 66, 73, 93, 94, 95, 105, 106
Swan Nebula 96

T

Tarantula Nebula 94
Taurus **76**, **77**, 96, 97, **99**
telescopes 5, 6, 7, 9, **14**, 15–16, **15**, 29, **29**
   alt-az mounting 16
   catadioptric refractor 15, **15**
   equatorial mounts 16
   Newtonian refractor 15, **15**
   refractor 15, **15**
   South Africa **16**
Tethys **40**
Thalassa 44
Theta Orionis **98**
Titan 18, **40**
   atmosphere 41
Titania 42
transits 22, 24, 25, 25, 26, 37, 75, 106
Trapezium Cluster **98**
Triangulum **69**, 97, **99**
Triangulum Australe 97, **99**
Trifid Nebula 96
Triton 44, **45**
   atmosphere 45
Tropic of Cancer **8**, 9
Tropic of Capricorn **8**, 9
Tucana 97, **99**, 104
Tycho (crater) 30, **31**

U

umbra 32, **32**
Umbriel 42
universe 4, 5, **10**, 11, 23, 69, 70, 71, 102, 104, 106
   expansion 72–73, **73**
Uranus 10, 19, **19**, 41, 42, **42**, **102**
   atmosphere 42
   rings 42
Ursa Major **78**, **79**, **99**
Ursa Minor **69**, **99**

V

Vega **9**, 52, **80**, **81**, **82**, **83**, 95, **100**
'Vela' 93, 97, **99**
Venus 10, 13, 18, **18**, 19, 22, **25**, 26–27, **26**, **27**, 29, **50**, 54, **102**, 103, 106
   phases 26
   temperature 27, 29
   transits 26–27
Vesta 50, 51
Virgo 69, 92, 97, **99**
Virgo Supercluster 69, 70, 92, 97
Vulpecula **65**, 97, **99**

W

water 37, 47, 51, 103
white dwarfs 29, 59, **62**, 63, **63**, 66, **66**, 93, 105, 106

Z

zodiacal light 54–55, **54**, 82, 106